PUZZLING PASSAGES

by
TRISHA FOOTE

PUZZLING PASSAGES

By

Trisha Foote

Copyright © 2024 Patricia Foote

The right of Patricia Foote to be identified as the author of this work has been asserted by her in accordance with the Copyright, Designs and Patents Act 1988.

All rights reserved. No part of this publication may be reproduced, stored in a retrieval system, or transmitted in any other form or by any means, electronic, mechanical, photocopying, recording or otherwise, without prior permission of the author.

ISBN 978-1-914388-65-1

Scripture quotations are taken from the Holy Bible,
New International Version (Anglicised edition).
Copyright © 1979, 1984, 2011 Biblica.
Used by permission of Hodder & Stoughton Ltd,
an Hachette UK company.
All rights reserved.
'NIV' is a registered trademark of Biblica.
UK trademark number 1448790.

Scripture quotations marked "ESV" are taken from the Holy Bible, English Standard Version (Anglicised). Published by HarperCollins Publishers © 2001 Crossway Bibles, a publishing ministry of Good News Publishers. Used by permission. All rights reserved.

Illustrations © 2024 Kate Hobbs

Print Management by Verité CM Ltd
www.veritecm.com

Printed in the UK

Contents

Intro 6

Perplexing Puzzles

1. Did a donkey really talk and why? 8
2. What did Jesus mean when he said, "Take the plank out of your eye"? .. 12
3. Can a camel go through the eye of a needle? 14
4. What does a bit and a rudder have to do with me? 16
5. How do we put on the armour of God? 19
6. How many times must I forgive someone? 24
7. How do I turn the other cheek? 27
8. Why was the widow giving more when she gave less? 29
9. Who was the fourth man in the fire? 32
10. How can we store up treasure in heaven? 35

Digging Deeper

11. Were there really giants on the earth? 38
12. How did Elijah prove God was real? 41
13. Why did the widow keep on knocking? 44
14. How do we pray? 46
15. Does God do bad things? 48
16. Should the elder son have been so jealous of his brother? 51
17. Did the sun really stand still and the moon stop moving? 54
18. Why did the prophets do weird things? 57
19. Should Jesus have been angry at the temple sellers? 61
20. Why did the man with one talent get it taken away? 65

Complicated Concepts

21. Why did Jesus say, "Eat Me"? 70
22. Does Jesus really want us to cut off our hand? 73
23. What does the number 666 stand for? 76
24. Should we really hate our parents? 80
25. What does it mean to carry your cross? 82
26. What did Jesus write on the ground? 85
27. Why did Jesus not condemn the shrewd manager? 88
28. What does it mean to "heap burning coals on their heads"? ...91
29. Can everyone who works for Jesus go to heaven? 93
30. Is there such a thing as an "unforgivable sin"? 96

Be your own Bible Detective! 98

Glossary 102

Helpful resources 108

Acknowledgements 109

Endorsements 110

About the Author 111

About the Illustrator... 111

Also by Trisha Foote 112

Dedication

I dedicate this book to the memory of Andy Mason
who had just written his first book,
was passionate about God and wanted to share the gospel.
May his legacy live on.

Intro

Hi!

Thank you for picking *Puzzling Passages*, and to those who have read my first book, *Gospel in a Nutshell*, welcome back!

Puzzling Passages came about because I remember how hard I found some parts of the Bible to understand. "How can a camel go through the eye of a needle?" I thought, and "How does a plank fit in your eye?" It all seemed a bit strange. So I set about writing this book to find out the answers to these tricky passages and, as you read it, I hope they will become clearer to you too. I am not an expert, but I do believe that with the help of the Holy Spirit and some good research I have made sense of some of the ones that have puzzled me over the years.

As in my last book, there are fascinating facts, and Kate has hidden some keys and gems in the illustrations for you to find. So, why keys and gems? Well they refer to two things I have put on each page.

Keys: These will help us unlock the passage. When we first look at a passage of scripture it can be very daunting, but when we have a key, we have something to guide us and help us to break it down in stages to make sense of it.

Gems: These will help us to live our lives in the right way. God doesn't want us to just read His Word, but He wants us to use what we learn to do our best for Him. The gems give us something we can take away from the passage and apply to our daily lives.

I've also included a section after the passages to help you become a Bible detective which will enable you to find your very own passages to unpick.

Enjoy solving the puzzling passages!

Trisha

PERPLEXING PUZZLES

Did a donkey really talk and why?

Numbers 22:27–33:

When the donkey saw the angel of the Lord, it lay down under Balaam, and he was angry and beat it with his staff. Then the Lord opened the donkey's mouth, and it said to Balaam, "What have I done to you to make you beat me these three times?"

Balaam answered the donkey, "You have made a fool of me! If only I had a sword in my hand, I would kill you right now."

The donkey said to Balaam, "Am I not your own donkey, which you have always ridden, to this day? Have I been in the habit of doing this to you?"

"No," he said.

Then the Lord opened Balaam's eyes, and he saw the angel of the Lord standing in the road with his sword drawn. So he bowed low and fell facedown.

The angel of the Lord asked him, "Why have you beaten your donkey these three times? I have come here to oppose you because your path is a reckless one before me. The donkey saw me and turned away from me these three times. If it had not turned away, I would certainly have killed you by now, but I would have spared it."

If, like me, you are a fan of Doctor Doolittle and Shrek, then this passage is very exciting! A talking donkey sounds amazing. But why *is* there a talking donkey in the Bible?

Key: God will use anything, even a donkey, to get our attention. It is helpful to read the whole passage, which starts at Numbers 22 verse 1. We can also find other passages in the Bible that can shed light on what is happening, such as in 2 Peter 2.

To find out the answer we have to look a bit deeper. In this passage there are three characters: the angel of the Lord; Balaam; the donkey.

Balaam is a prophet (that is a man who hears from God), and I have to tell you that there were good and bad prophets in the Old Testament and, unfortunately, Balaam was a bad prophet. He was asked by a wicked king, called Balak, to curse God's people the Israelites, because he was scared of them. The king had heard of how the Israelites had already defeated the Amorites. Now God told Balaam not to curse them so he refused to do what the king asked.

I think I ought to explain what a curse is here. When the Israelites were following God and obeying Him, He blessed them by looking after them and giving them peace with their neighbours. But when they disobeyed God then He cursed them by taking away His protection and peace. God was their Father and He didn't want to hurt them but He needed to discipline them so they would learn to follow Him.

Then Balak, who was king of Moab, asked him again and this time he promised him a lot of money, so Balaam asked God again. This time God allowed him to go, as long as he only said what God told him to say. It was on this journey that the angel appeared.

Seeing the angel of the Lord would have been very scary, and the donkey, who had faithfully served Balaam, only did what was right. But Balaam couldn't see the angel and got very angry with the donkey, to the point of wanting to kill it! This reveals his true character, which wasn't godly at all, but only wanting to serve his own self. God was angry with Balaam and wanted to stop him on his journey. When he didn't, God used the donkey to tell him off.

So did the donkey talk? It seems more likely that God spoke through the donkey. If we look at **2 Peter 2:16** it says:

But he was rebuked for his wrongdoing by a donkey – an animal without speech – who spoke with a human voice and restrained the prophet's madness

This seems very clear to me that it wasn't the donkey's actual voice

but it did come out of its mouth. It's a very strange situation and the oddest thing of all is that Balaam carried on having a conversation with the donkey as if it was perfectly normal! Sometimes when people are very angry the emotion of it all makes them do things that are not rational!

So what can we learn from this bizarre episode? Balaam wanted to do things his way and not God's. The bottom line is that God didn't want Balaam to go, but Balaam kept pushing God, so in the end He let him go. God will often do that to us too. It was in His mercy that God stopped Balaam and talked to him rather than take his life. We have to remember that God is holy and just (being morally right and fair) and will not be used as a tool to get our own way. Israel was God's holy and blessed people and He was protecting them. So when we do things we need to listen to God and do things His way and not ours.

Fascinating Fact: Donkeys are mentioned a lot in the Bible. They are intelligent and have a good sense of survival. They won't do anything that might put them in danger, which is why this donkey probably refused to go any further. This action can make them seem stubborn, hence the saying, "stubborn as a mule" (a mule is a cross between a donkey and a horse).

In the end Balaam did say sorry to God and he listened to God for a while and refused to curse the Israelites, even when offered lots of money. But craftily he showed Balak a way to get the Israelites to sin themselves by finding other gods, so then God had to curse them by taking away their blessing.

Gem: If we do wander away from what God wants us to do, He will guide us back, sometimes in ways we won't expect. It is best to accept what God wants for us and not to push if He says no. We will be better off going His way rather than our way.

What did Jesus mean when he said, "Take the plank out of your eye"?

Matthew 7:3–5:

"Why do you look at the speck of sawdust in your brother's eye and pay no attention to the plank in your own eye? How can you say to your brother, 'Let me take the speck out of your eye,' when all the time there is a plank in your own eye? You hypocrite, first take the plank out of your own eye, and then you will see clearly to remove the speck from your brother's eye."

This is one of the passages that I found very confusing when I was young. What on earth was Jesus talking about?

Key: To make sense of it, we first have to read the verse before it and that will give us a big clue. It talks about not judging people and that is the key that unlocks this verse. So if we say that the verse is about judging people and looking at their faults instead of our own, then it makes sense!

Firstly, we have to ask what is a plank? It is a long piece of wood and it would certainly be impossible to put one in your eye! A speck of sawdust is literally a tiny piece of wood dust that could get in your eye, and it would be a bit irritating if it did. Secondly, if it is impossible to get a plank in your eye, why would Jesus say it?

I have to say, I think it is interesting that Jesus mentions wood in this passage as he was himself a carpenter and would have made a lot of items out of wood. In the Bible Jesus often talked about familiar things, and people listening to Him would have understood what a plank and a speck were and could have connected it to their everyday lives.

As we have seen in the key, this puzzling passage is about us judging people and looking at their faults instead of our own, thinking we are better than them and sometimes even believing we are perfect! The plank, then, is the big fault in us and the little speck is the fault in our family and friends.

This is a big deal! Which is why Jesus mentioned it. We never like to own up to our own faults; we look past them and often blame our negative behaviour on others. We can minimise our faults and make other people's bigger in our own eyes. Besides, it is not right to look down on others and Jesus doesn't want us to have this stinking attitude. Also, we should make sure we are not in the wrong before we go accusing other people. Otherwise we could end up looking foolish!

So how can we sort out this problem? Stepping back and looking at the situation as a whole, remembering that we have faults too, is a good way to begin. Then we are in a good place to help others. Jesus said to remove your fault first, then you can help the other person with an attitude of love and humility. Not an easy task, and we need to ask Him to help us.

Gem: We must not be judgemental, and remember that no-one is perfect, not even us!

Fascinating Fact:

The largest tree in the world is called the giant sequoia tree, also called the General Sherman tree. It can be over 80-metres high and 30-metres wide.

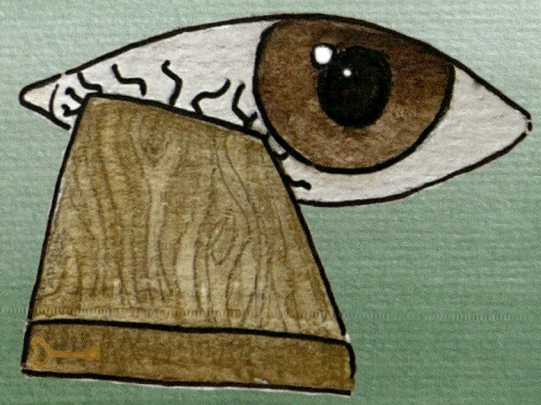

Can a camel go through the eye of a needle?

> **Matthew 19:23–24:**
>
> Then Jesus said to his disciples, "Truly I tell you, it is hard for someone who is rich to enter the kingdom of heaven. Again I tell you, it is easier for a camel to go through the eye of a needle than for someone who is rich to enter the kingdom of God."

I have quite a vivid imagination and I remember picturing in my mind a camel trying to squeeze through the eye of the needle (that's the bit the thread goes through at the top of the needle). Of course it's impossible! So what is Jesus telling His followers, the disciples?

Key: It is hard for someone who is rich to enter the kingdom of God. We need to look at the verses before this one to help us, and also understand that it is the *love* of money, rather than *having* money, that is the issue.

To tackle this passage we have to begin by looking at the verses before it – **Matthew 19:16–22**. It starts with a young man who asks Jesus how he can get to heaven and have eternal life. Jesus asks him if he has obeyed all the commandments God set out, and he says he has done that. Then Jesus tells him to sell everything he has and follow Him. The young man was very sad and walked away from Jesus as he had tons of money and couldn't bring himself to give it all away. I think we would all struggle with that!

God clearly tells us in the Bible that the *love* of money is the root of all evil. We can have money but we can't serve two masters: God and money. The key word here is *love*. I don't think God would tell us to give away money unless it's a problem for us. If our heart is set on building a kingdom or empire here on earth then we don't have our hearts set on building God's kingdom. It's a tough call to give away everything you have but maybe the young man loved his money more than God, and Jesus would have known this.

So, back to the camel. There are many theories about what Jesus was comparing the camel and the needle to. Some people think there was a gate in Jerusalem that was so low the camels struggled to get through it, or that the word is "cable" not "camel", meaning a thick rope, which would be impossible to get through a small eye. Or He could have been quoting a Jewish idiom (idioms are phrases and sayings that don't mean what they say, like "it's raining cats and dogs").

Whatever the reason, the point Jesus is making is that people who have lots of money need to make sure that it isn't stopping them from loving God. Money can puff us up with pride and make us think we are better than poor people. Like the camel who would have to bow low to get through the gate, rich people need to be humble and realise they are not superior to others. The irony is that God could have replaced the money the young man gave away because nothing is impossible for God. Or he may have actually had a better life without all the trappings that money can bring.

After Jesus had said this, the disciples were gobsmacked! They said, "How is this possible?" They were thinking, how can rich people be saved and get into heaven? As we have seen, God can do anything, but we have to do our part too. We have to put God first in all things, then everything else will work out for the best for us.

Gem: We must not let money, or anything we love, get in the way of our relationship with God.

Fascinating Fact: Camels have three sets of eyelids and two sets of eyelashes to keep out the sand from the desert in which they live.

What does a bit and a rudder have to do with me?

James 3:2–5:

We all stumble in many ways. Anyone who is never at fault in what they say is perfect, able to keep their whole body in check. When we put bits into the mouths of horses to make them obey us, we can turn the whole animal. Or take ships as an example. Although they are so large and are driven by strong winds, they are steered by a very small rudder wherever the pilot wants to go. Likewise, the tongue is a small part of the body, but it makes great boasts.

This passage used to make me smile as I conjured up wild horses and boats sailing on stormy seas but I couldn't quite understand what it meant. What have horses and boats got to do with me?

Key: The passage tells us that we need to keep our bodies in check and that the tongue is small but makes great boasts.

This is not as complicated as it first looks. As with most Bible passages, if we break it down into smaller chunks the treasure within can be revealed.

If you think about a horse, at first they are wild and have to be broken in. They have to get used to wearing a bridle and saddle if they are to be ridden. So that the rider can be in control there is a bit (a piece of metal attached to the bridle) that goes into the horse's mouth, and with it the rider makes the horse go where they want it to go.

It's the same with the ship. The rudder is a small metal flap with a hinge with which the captain guides the boat in the direction they want it to go. James tells us that it is the same with us; our tongues might be small but they can steer us in the wrong direction too. We can let our tongues get out of control and say things that are mean and false. We can say a lot of bad things with our tongues and a lot of friendships can be broken by what we say.

We don't have a "bit" or a "rudder" so how do we control our tongues? At the beginning of the passage, it talks about keeping our body in check. When we keep something "in check" it means that we are aware of it and make it do what we want. When we love God we want to do what is right and that includes how we speak. We can ask the Holy Spirit for love and self-control. The fruit is what God gives us to help us in our Christian walk.

Galatians 5:22–23:

But the fruit of the Spirit is love, joy, peace, forbearance, kindness, goodness, faithfulness, gentleness and self-control.

We can pray to God and ask Him to help us "guard our mouths" and help us not to speak unkind things.

Psalm 141:3:

Set a guard over my mouth, Lord; keep watch over the door of my lips.

It is important that we think about what we are going to say before we say it. This includes: saying hateful and hurtful things, lying, gossiping, and criticising others. If we think before we speak, act in love and pray, then we should be able to control our tongues. There will be times when we make a mistake and then we can always say sorry and apologise.

Gem: Pray and ask God to help us to think before we speak, and act in love and self-control.

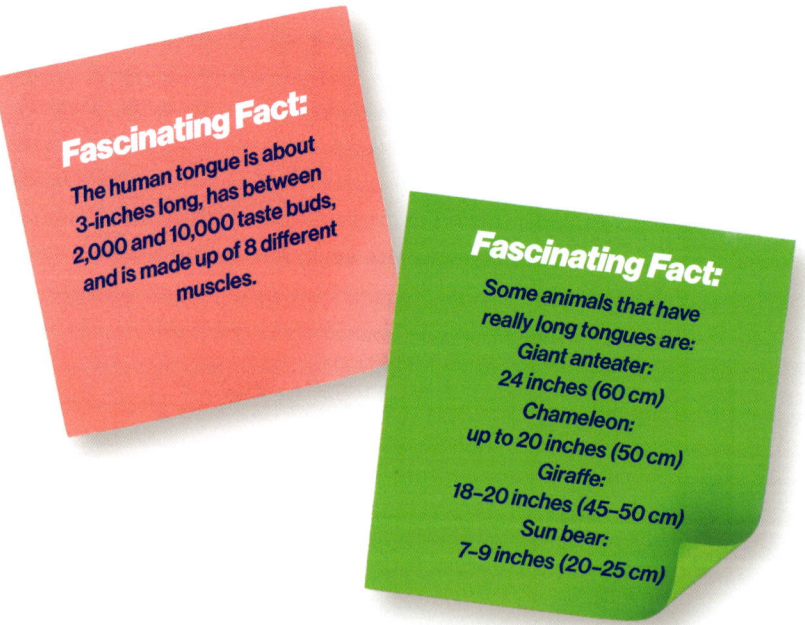

Fascinating Fact:
The human tongue is about 3-inches long, has between 2,000 and 10,000 taste buds, and is made up of 8 different muscles.

Fascinating Fact:
Some animals that have really long tongues are:
Giant anteater:
24 inches (60 cm)
Chameleon:
up to 20 inches (50 cm)
Giraffe:
18–20 inches (45–50 cm)
Sun bear:
7–9 inches (20–25 cm)

How do we put on the armour of God?

Ephesians 6:13–17:

Therefore put on the full armour of God, so that when the day of evil comes, you may be able to stand your ground, and after you have done everything, to stand. Stand firm then, with the belt of truth buckled around your waist, with the breastplate of righteousness in place, and with your feet fitted with the readiness that comes from the gospel of peace. In addition to all this, take up the shield of faith, with which you can extinguish all the flaming arrows of the evil one. Take the helmet of salvation and the sword of the Spirit, which is the word of God.

Can you imagine having a special suit to protect you, even better than the one Iron Man wears? How exciting would that be? Well, believe it or not we can have one!

Key: We need to put on the armour of God to protect us from evil and to fight the enemy, the devil.

When we become a Christian we enter the battle between good and evil, but it's not a physical battle, it's a spiritual one. So, just like Iron Man, when a soldier goes into battle he wears armour and it's no different for a Christian. Now the man who wrote this passage, Paul, would have seen Roman soldiers walking around and based this passage on them to show Christians how to protect themselves.

The superheroes we enjoy watching, whether it's Superman, Batman, Spiderman, to name but a few, they all fight evil and it's no different with the spiritual world. We are in a battle with the devil and his demons. They are real and what they want more than anything is to trip you up and get you to fail and give up. We all have doubts, worries, guilt and shame. When bad thoughts come into our mind it becomes a battlefield and we have to fight them or they will pull us down.

The Bible tells us in **1 Peter 5:8** that:

[Our] enemy the devil prowls around like a roaring lion looking for someone to devour.

Once we become a Christian we become a target but God doesn't leave us without any help. He sends us the Holy Spirit and He clothes us just like the superheroes – then we can fight, not in our strength but in His. Don't be scared though, because God is much more powerful than the devil and the Bible tells us not to fear him, just to be prepared.

So how do we put this armour on? This was always a big puzzle for me! We can't see the armour, so it would be impossible, wouldn't it?

First, we need to see that the battle is a spiritual one: we are fighting an invisible army! As a Christian we can feel pressured into doing things we'd rather not do – we can be tempted by our friends or we might want to fit into a group because we don't want to stand out. So we need protecting from the bad stuff around us and from doing wrong things. We call this "sin" and we need help to resist it.

Second, it's a case of knowing what each piece is and learning to put them all into practice. Some say put it on every day and some say once it's on it stays on! But it's more about understanding, so we can use each piece to protect us.

The Bible passage starts with the belt of truth, probably because it is very important to know that Jesus is the truth, but I'm working from the head down to the feet to keep it simple.

It might help you to imagine each piece going on as you read it:

Helmet of salvation

We need to know that we belong to Jesus (that's salvation) and fully give our lives to Him. When our mind gets attacked by thoughts and doubts, we have to remember that God loves us (because He can't do anything else – He *is* love) and that what we read in the Bible is true. This will help us to live our lives in a godly way.

Breastplate of righteousness

The breastplate covers the chest of the person, including the heart. As Christians we need to protect our hearts from sin and from making bad decisions. We can do this by making the right choices, but even when we get it wrong we can say sorry to God. It is wonderful to know that we can be forgiven when we fail and that God can make us right with Him again.

Belt of truth

Truth is the opposite of lies. The Bible tells us that the devil is the father of all lies. It also tells us that Jesus is the way, the *truth* and the life. The meaning of "truth" is: reality, a fact. So therefore, it is a fact that Jesus is truth and He can let us know what is true. In a practical way, we must also be honest and truthful too.

Shield of faith

A shield was lifted up to cover the soldier from the enemy's arrows. We can use it to protect ourselves when doubts come to try and knock our faith by asking God to increase and strengthen our faith. We know we can trust God as He is faithful and true. The shield also enables us to walk forward in difficult circumstances.

We can also speak the Bible out loud to increase our faith, such as the following verse:

Psalm 119:114:

You are my refuge and shield, I have put my hope in your word.

Sword of the Spirit

This is a weapon we use not just to defend ourselves but to attack the enemy too. The best way to attack is with the Word of God, our Bible. When Jesus was in the desert the devil tried to tempt Him with bread because He was hungry, and with power, to own the world instead of having to go to the cross. Jesus answered him with the Word of God. You can read this in **Matthew: 3–10**. The second use of the sword is with God's Spirit. When we accept Jesus into our hearts, the Holy Spirit lives within us. We can ask Him to help us and to live our lives in the correct way. With the sword we can cut off anything that is getting in the way of our walk with God.

Shoes of readiness – the gospel of peace

We must be ready at all times to tell people about Jesus and sometimes that means God can take us to places we would never have dreamed of going. Missionaries in the past have been guided to go to China, Africa and India, to name but a few. Sometimes it's where we are, in our home town or village. Saint Francis de Sales said, "Bloom where you're planted!" In this chaotic world we can bring peace to others, the peace which only Jesus can give.

Fascinating Fact: In the Middle Ages a suit of armour was not as heavy as you think. They weighed 15–25 kg. That's less than what a soldier would wear today. Some people thought that a soldier in a suit of armour had to be lifted on to his horse by a crane!

John 14:27:

Peace I leave with you; my peace I give you. I do not give to you as the world gives. Do not let your hearts be troubled and do not be afraid.

Now we can see from this list that our back is exposed. Yes, we are to move forward all the time in our Christian walk but when I prayed about this God gave me this scripture:

Isaiah 52:12:

But you will not leave in haste or go in flight; for the LORD will go before you, the God of Israel will be your rear guard.

Isn't that great? God has your back!

At the beginning of the passage it says "stand". When we've done all we can, we just stay still and God will fight our battles for us. How amazing is that?

Fascinating Fact: Roman soldiers carried shields that were covered with heavy animal hide. Before a battle they would dip their shields in water so that when the fiery arrows hit them, the wet animal hide would put them out.

Gem: We need to wear our armour so that we can be protected from evil and also be effective as Christians.

How many times must I forgive someone?

Matthew 18:21–22:

Then Peter came to Jesus and asked, "Lord, how many times shall I forgive my brother or sister who sins against me? Up to seven times?"

Jesus answered, "I tell you, not seven times, but seventy-seven times."

I love Peter! He was the disciple who really got to the centre of things. He'd obviously been thinking about it and realising that maybe forgiving people once was not enough, he'd gone out on a limb and said seven. I often think he said things that the other disciples thought but weren't brave enough to say!

Key: After these verses is a parable about a king who forgives his servant but then his servant doesn't forgive another man and gets put into prison. After Jesus told this parable he ended with:

"This is how my heavenly Father will treat each of you unless you forgive your brother or sister from your heart."

Can forgiveness be boiled down to a simple mathematics formula? Of course not! Peter thought he was being very generous when he was saying seven times. I bet in his head he was thinking a smaller number, but knowing Jesus, he thought he ought to be more generous and said seven. Surely that would be enough! You can imagine Peter's face when he heard Jesus's reply! No, Peter, not seven, but seventy-

Fascinating Fact:
The rabbis (teachers) in Jesus's time said three times was enough to forgive, so Peter was being generous. Interestingly, the number seven is seen as God's number of perfection and completion.

seven times. Some versions of the Bible say seventy times seven! That would be 490 times to forgive someone!

So what does all this mean? If someone, anyone – a friend or enemy – upsets you, or hurts you in some way, you have to forgive them. Not just in words but in your heart. You have to treat it the same way God does. He doesn't hold a grudge, bringing it up every time we do something else wrong. Remember when you did something very bad, maybe you hit someone or stole something? If we say sorry to God then that incident has gone from His memory.

How do we feel when we are hurt? We experience lots of negative feelings such as anger, frustration, injustice, anxiety, even depression. To forgive someone when we feel like that is tough and we might say that once is enough, but seven would be pretty difficult to do, let alone 490 times! Forgiveness is hard!

So how do we do it? Firstly, we can't do it without Jesus and the Holy Spirit. If we love God we want to walk in love, because God is love. That means getting on with people as much as we can and saying sorry and allowing them to say sorry. Sometimes we even have to forgive ourselves. That can be just as hard, if not harder, than forgiving others.

Secondly, we have to remember that God said several times in the Bible that we *must* forgive – it isn't optional – because He has forgiven us. Many people have described unforgiveness as taking poison yourself hoping the other person will die. We hold on to the bitterness and anger and, in so doing, we are hurting ourselves, while often the other person isn't even aware of it.

> **Fascinating Fact:**
> Unforgiveness can affect our body by pushing up our blood pressure, affecting our sleep, making us stressed and having stomach problems. It's as bad for our health as it is our spiritual life.

How do we do it? We come to God, our Father, and say that we forgive that person, not in our own strength, but in His. It is something that we have to actively do.

I remember God reminding me of an incident that had happened many years before, and even though I had forgotten about it, when I thought of that person I still felt anger towards them. I knew that God was telling me to forgive them. So I said to God, "I forgive [name of person you are forgiving] not in my strength but in Yours. Please help me to not carry this grudge, but help me to let it go." And do you know what, He did. Whenever I think of this person now, I have no anger at all. The poison has left my system. In its place is peace.

One other thing to remember is that you may forget what this person has done or you may not. It is not about excusing the harm that has been done to you or even making up with the other person. In fact, forgiving someone isn't saying that what they did was ok, it's about taking them off our hook and placing them onto God's hook. Every circumstance is different and God will show you if there is anything else He wants you to do. It's all about not holding it in your heart and living in torment. Being in unforgiveness can be like being in prison, and that's something we don't want and God doesn't want for us either.

Let us give Corrie ten Boom the last word: "God buries our sins in the depths of the sea and then puts up a sign that reads, 'No fishing.'"

Gem: We need to walk in love and forgiveness. Forgiveness is hard and we need God's help to do it.

How do I turn the other cheek?

Matthew 5:38–42:

"You have heard that it was said, 'Eye for eye, and tooth for tooth.' But I tell you, do not resist an evil person. If anyone slaps you on the right cheek, turn to them the other cheek also. And if anyone wants to sue you and take your shirt, hand over your coat as well. If anyone forces you to go one mile, go with them two miles. Give to the one who asks you, and do not turn away from the one who wants to borrow from you."

This passage seems to say that we should be treated badly by others, but I don't think Jesus would say that, would He?

Key: We need to compare other verses in the Bible that talk about the same subject and remember that God wants us to do the right thing.

It's quite a well-known saying "to turn the other cheek" but what does it actually mean? Are we going to let people who hit us, do it again? In Jewish Law, if someone took your tooth, you could take one of theirs. This wasn't usually taken literally but if someone lost a tooth they could have the value of it in money. It was really given more as a guide so that Jewish people didn't take their own revenge.

Matthew 5:44 says:

But I tell you, love your enemies and pray for those who persecute you.

Love your enemies! Well, I hear you say, why should I love people who are horrible to me? When Jesus asks us to do something, it can be difficult and we want to resist it, especially if it doesn't make sense. This is why the religious people in His day found it hard to understand Him because He was turning all they believed upside down! Let's dig a bit deeper. Think about Jesus: His whole life was about serving others and in the end He gave up His life for us all. If He was prepared to give up everything then we should follow His example. Putting others before ourselves isn't easy but it is possible if we ask God to help us.

If we think about a situation where someone comes up to us and calls us names, it is tempting to call them names back or do something worse, like spread a rumour about them. But Jesus says no, don't be like them, be the best person you can be. If you do call them names then the whole thing could get worse and may even get out of hand.

But if you don't say anything, or even try and be nice back to them, they will get a shock! That wouldn't be what they would be expecting! They might even end up being a friend.

In **1 Thessalonians 5:15** it says:

Make sure that nobody pays back wrong for wrong, but always strive to do what is good for each other and for everyone else.

Fascinating Fact: If a tooth gets knocked out of your mouth it will start to die within 5 minutes. You can preserve it by putting it in milk, but only for about an hour.

A few years ago someone borrowed a camera off me and my husband and then ruined it by dropping it in the sea! I really wanted to get them to pay for it but I felt God say to me, no, don't ask them. Just leave it. I didn't want to but I knew deep down this was the right thing to do. You see, if I'd asked them to replace it then they may not have, and it might have drifted on for months or even years and it could have turned into a feud. This way I could move on. It might not seem fair, but God can more than make up for it. He could replace it with a better item or He could be showing us how to live a more Christian life.

Have you had a time when you felt hard done by or wanted to get back at someone? Do you think you would now react differently from the way you did then? The more we do the right thing the easier it will become.

Gem: God wants us to be humble, to love others and not seek to defend ourselves but let Him do that for us.

Why was the widow giving more when she gave less?

Mark 12:41–44:

Jesus sat down opposite the place where the offerings were put and watched the crowd putting their money into the temple treasury. Many rich people threw in large amounts. But a poor widow came and put in two very small copper coins, worth only a few pence.

Calling his disciples to him, Jesus said, "Truly I tell you, this poor widow has put more into the treasury than all the others. They all gave out of their wealth; but she, out of her poverty, put in everything – all she had to live on."

Again another conundrum! You have lots of rich people putting loads of money into a pot for the temple, then a widow comes along, giving a very small amount, and Jesus said she had given more!

Key: It looks as though it's about money until you see that Jesus is talking more about the state of their hearts.

At first this looks like a really tricky passage, but the second paragraph shows us the key. Let's look at what was happening. Jesus was sitting with His disciples watching people put their money into the offering jar. They must have seen a lot of money being placed in there by rich people who could easily afford to part with some cash, and have lots left over. Then this poor widow put in everything that she had, which was just a few small coins. I should imagine that no one else but God had noticed her offering. She had truly given everything she had, there was nothing left. Can you think what that would be like? That she would go home, maybe not even having enough to eat? We don't know why she did it, and what her motive was, but she must have loved God so much that she wanted to give it all to Him.

You might wonder how Jesus knew it was all she had, but we have to remember that Jesus is God too, not just a man, and full of the Holy Spirit, so He would have known. God knows things that we don't know and He can tell us if He wants to.

So what lesson does God want us to learn from this? Jesus often talked about the Pharisees and the religious people as doing things so that

Why was the widow giving more when she gave less?

Mark 12:41–44:

Jesus sat down opposite the place where the offerings were put and watched the crowd putting their money into the temple treasury. Many rich people threw in large amounts. But a poor widow came and put in two very small copper coins, worth only a few pence.

Calling his disciples to him, Jesus said, "Truly I tell you, this poor widow has put more into the treasury than all the others. They all gave out of their wealth; but she, out of her poverty, put in everything – all she had to live on."

Again another conundrum! You have lots of rich people putting loads of money into a pot for the temple, then a widow comes along, giving a very small amount, and Jesus said she had given more!

Key: It looks as though it's about money until you see that Jesus is talking more about the state of their hearts.

At first this looks like a really tricky passage, but the second paragraph shows us the key. Let's look at what was happening. Jesus was sitting with His disciples watching people put their money into the offering jar. They must have seen a lot of money being placed in there by rich people who could easily afford to part with some cash, and have lots left over. Then this poor widow put in everything that she had, which was just a few small coins. I should imagine that no one else but God had noticed her offering. She had truly given everything she had, there was nothing left. Can you think what that would be like? That she would go home, maybe not even having enough to eat? We don't know why she did it, and what her motive was, but she must have loved God so much that she wanted to give it all to Him.

You might wonder how Jesus knew it was all she had, but we have to remember that Jesus is God too, not just a man, and full of the Holy Spirit, so He would have known. God knows things that we don't know and He can tell us if He wants to.

So what lesson does God want us to learn from this? Jesus often talked about the Pharisees and the religious people as doing things so that

others could see what they were doing, but this was not pleasing to God. Anyone can give when they have loads left over, but few will give when it is everything that they have. That means real sacrifice.

Let me tell you what God showed me many years ago. When I first became a Christian I resented putting money in the collection. I didn't have much money and I thought, why am I giving what I don't have to the vicar? Well, God spoke deep into my heart! He showed me that I wasn't giving the money to the vicar or the church, but to Him. Now, God doesn't need our money but He does want us to serve Him and His church, and sometimes that means giving what we have, whether it is money or time or our gifts and talents. The church and Christian missions and charities wouldn't be able to move forward without them.

> **Fascinating Fact:**
> There were four coins that Jesus and His disciples would have definitely come into contact with: the shekel, half-shekel, the lepton and the denarius. The lepton was a small, almost worthless, poor-quality bronze coin. These were most likely to have been the coins that the widow put into the offering.

The Bible tells us in **2 Corinthians 9:7**:

Each of you should give what you have decided in your heart to give, not reluctantly or under compulsion, for God loves a cheerful giver.

In other words, we should give to God because we want to, not because we are forced to by others or because we feel guilty or want to show off, and we should do it cheerfully.

I'll finish with a funny story that happened to me a few years ago. My neighbour phoned and asked if I could give her a toilet roll as she had run out. I gave her my last one and, even though I did so happily, I was sort of worried that I didn't now have one once I had finished my roll.

Well, when I came back from my visit, there on the doorstep was a toilet roll! It was from a company giving out free toilet roll samples. God had honoured my giving and in so doing He also made me smile. How we are blessed when we do what God wants us to do.

Gem: It is good to give to God but we must do it cheerfully and with a willing heart. It is important to do it with the right motive and not to do it to feel important.

Who was the fourth man in the fire?

Daniel 3:22–27:

The king's command was so urgent and the furnace so hot that the flames of the fire killed the soldiers who took up Shadrach, Meshach and Abednego, and these three men, firmly tied, fell into the blazing furnace.

Then King Nebuchadnezzar leaped to his feet in amazement and asked his advisors, "Weren't there three men that we tied up and threw into the fire?"

They replied, "Certainly, Your Majesty."

He said, "Look! I see four men walking around in the fire, unbound and unharmed, and the fourth looks like a son of the gods."

Nebuchadnezzar then approached the opening of the blazing furnace and shouted, "Shadrach, Meshach and Abednego, servants of the Most High God, come out! Come here!"

So Shadrach, Meshach and Abednego came out of the fire, and the satraps, prefects, governors and royal advisors crowded around them. They saw that the fire had not harmed their bodies, nor was a hair of their heads singed; their robes were not scorched and there was no smell of fire on them.

What an exciting story! It could so easily have been titled, "Why did they not burn up?" It has such powerful imagery, and I love the names. I used to call Abednego, A-bed-we-go! To survive a furnace so hot that it killed the men putting them into it is incredible, but to have a fourth man walking around in there adds to the mystery. Who was he?

Key: The fourth looks like a son of the gods.

To understand it fully, I will give you some background. King Nebuchadnezzar (that's not easy to say!) made a big statue of gold and

told everyone to bow down and worship it. If they didn't, then they would be put into the fiery furnace. Some of his astrologers told him that there were three Jewish men who worked for him, who only worshipped their own God and wouldn't bow down to the statue.

The king was so furious that he summoned the men and asked them if this was true and they said yes. He asked them, "What god will be able to rescue you from my hand?"

Incredibly, he is saying that he is more powerful than God, and that is a dangerous thing to do! These brave men answered him, "King Nebuchadnezzar, we do not need to defend ourselves before you in this matter. If we are thrown into the blazing furnace, the God we serve is able to deliver us from it, and he will deliver us from Your Majesty's hand. But even if he does not, we want you to know, Your Majesty, that we will not serve your gods or worship the image of gold you have set up" (**Daniel 3:15–18**).

Wow! I don't know if I would have been so brave if I had been in their shoes but they stood firm, even if it meant going into the fire. When they were thrown into the fire the ropes that tied them came off and they started walking around. What also astounds me is the fact that when they came out they weren't burnt in any way and didn't smell of fire.

So let's answer the question of who is the fourth man. The clue "he looks like a son of the gods" shows us that he didn't have the same appearance as a normal man. There was something special about him, and even though this story was in the Old Testament when they didn't know about Jesus, I believe it was Jesus in there with them. The Bible tells us He has been with the Father (God) from the beginning. He is also known as the Son of God. Some people think it was an angel in there with them. Whichever it was, we know that God was protecting them from certain death.

The ending is just as amazing as the king then declares that no-one can say anything bad against God or they will be killed, because "no other god can save in this way" (verse 29).

Gem: We have to stand firm in our faith, whatever we come up against. God will be with us even if the outcome isn't what we want.

How can we store up treasure in heaven?

Matthew 6:19–21:

Do not store up for yourselves treasures on earth, where moths and vermin destroy, and where thieves break in and steal. But store up for yourselves treasures in heaven, where moths and vermin do not destroy, and where thieves do not break in and steal. For where your treasure is, there your heart will be also.

It's easy to understand that things can be stolen on earth but how can we store things up in heaven? We can't get up there to put things in, can we?

Key: The key here is that your treasure is where your heart is.

Sadly, many people have had their houses broken into. It's a horrible experience that can leave emotional scars. Some people lose sentimental things that they were given by loved ones. Rich people go to great lengths to protect their homes and belongings and, even then, they can still have their things taken.

It makes sense that Jesus says don't build up your treasures where they can be stolen, or they can be eaten up by rats or moths. This actually happened to a friend of mine. She had her precious collection of records and other items stored in her garage. After many years she went to look at them and they had been gnawed at by rats – there was a lot of wee and poo too! You wouldn't want your stuff after that.

The question asks how can we store up treasure in heaven? Firstly, we have to ask, what is the treasure that Jesus is talking about? Well it can't be material things like PlayStations and dolls as it would be impossible to put them in heaven. There wouldn't be a ladder tall enough! Have a think – what do you love most? Whatever we treasure will be in our hearts. You know if someone has a favourite hobby or toy as they talk about it a lot. It's ok to have a hobby or toy but it shouldn't be first place in our lives. If we love God we will want to do things that make Him happy, such as doing kind things and telling our friends about Him.

Jesus is telling us that if we love our things, which can go rotten or get stolen, then we love them more than God. He wants us to love what He loves, and when we go to heaven we won't want our things that are left behind but we will have Him forever. So it makes sense to love Him and serve Him now while we are on the earth and, wow, what treasure we will have in heaven!

Gem: Our things on earth won't last, but if we put our trust in heavenly things they will last forever.

Fascinating Fact: Under the Treasure Act, coins are not considered to be treasure until they are 300 years old.

DIGGING DEEPER

Were there really giants on the earth?

1 Samuel 17:4:

A champion named Goliath, who was from Gath, came out of the Philistine camp. His height was six cubits and a span.

When I was a child and watched *Jack and the Beanstalk* I thought giants were made-up creatures. But when I read in the Bible about a young man called David defeating a giant called Goliath, I wondered, did giants actually exist on the earth?

Key: Looking at other passages that talk about giants and knowing that the Bible is a factual document.

Giants are an exciting part of fairy tales and get our imagination going! But if we are totally honest we are glad that they don't really exist, aren't we? But what if they did? I think it would have been scary but the Bible tells us that they were around in days gone by.

We can see that Goliath was not only tall – six cubits and a span is about 9 feet 9 inches tall (2.97 metres) – but strong too. His coat of armour weighed over 90lbs (41 kilograms), which is about the same as a new calf!

So was Goliath the only giant mentioned in the Bible? No! There are many examples but here are a few:

Deuteronomy 3:11: Og, king of Bashan, was the last of the Rephaites. His bed was decorated with iron and was more than nine cubits long and four cubits wide.

That's about 4.1 metres by 1.8 metres or 13.5 feet by 6 feet!

> **Fascinating Fact:**
> The tallest man in recent times was Robert Wadlow. He was 8 feet 11 inches (2.72 metres) tall.

2 Samuel 21:16: Then Ishbi-Benob, one of the descendants of Rapha, whose bronze spearhead weighed three hundred shekels and who was armed with a new sword, said he would kill David.

That meant that his spearhead weighed over 7 pounds (3.2 kilograms) in weight. Both Og and Ishbi-Benob were Rephaites, which means "terrible ones". They were strong and ferocious fighters, tall and imposing. How brave was David to stand up to Goliath!

2 Samuel 21:20: There was a huge man with six fingers on each hand and six toes on each foot – twenty-four in all.

So what does the word "giant" mean? It is a being with human form but with superhuman size and strength. The clue could be in the word "superhuman".

So where did these giants come from? The Bible tells us about the Nephilim.

Genesis 6:4: The Nephilim were on the earth in those days – and also afterwards – when the sons of God went to the daughters of humans and had children by them. They were the heroes of old, men of renown.

Numbers 13:32–33: All the people we saw there are of great size. We saw the Nephilim there (the descendants of Anak come from the Nephilim). We seemed like grasshoppers in our own eyes, and we looked the same to them.

Reading this, we have to ask the question, who were the descendants of Anak, who came from the Nephilim? Well, they were a race of people who lived in Canaan and were driven out by the Israelites. Here's what the

Bible says about them:

Deuteronomy 9:2: The people are strong and tall – Anakites! You know about them and have heard it said: "Who can stand up against the Anakites?"

In the first passage we read about the Nephilim (which means "fallen ones") who are talked about in the Bible. So who are the Nephilim?

Just before the flood the Bible tells us the earth became wicked and the sons of God married women and had babies with them. It is possible that they were "fallen angels" – angels that had fallen to earth with Satan when he was kicked out of heaven. Some people refer to:

2 Peter 2:4: For if God did not spare angels when they sinned, but sent them to hell, putting them in chains of darkness to be held for judgement.

The angels must have done something really bad, and marrying women on the earth would be bad as angels were not created by God to marry humans.

So how do we pull this all together? Just from the Bible verses we can see that there were some very tall, strong people around in early times. It's unclear if they were all bad but some had a proud attitude, such as Goliath. They may have come from fallen angels and this would explain their abnormal height and strength. As far as I know, there aren't any around these days!

We all have "giants" in our lives, whether they be a bully, a fight with your family or friends, fear and worry, or an addiction to something – maybe a computer game! Whatever we face we can fight it with God's help. David was a good example. He was not afraid because he knew that God was with him. Often the fear of something is worse than actually confronting it. So we can learn from this that whatever battles we fight we can depend on God for our strength to defeat them.

Gem: Whatever "giants" we are facing in our lives, we can know for sure that God is looking after us and He is in control.

How did Elijah prove God was real?

1 Kings 18:22–24:

Then Elijah said to them, "I am the only one of the Lord's prophets left, but Baal has four hundred and fifty prophets. Get two bulls for us. Let Baal's prophets choose one for themselves, and let them cut it into pieces and put it on the wood but not set fire to it. I will prepare the other bull and put it on the wood but not set fire to it. Then you call on the name of your god, and I will call on the name of the Lord. The god who answers by fire – he is God."

The question that everyone asks at some point in their lives is how do I know God is real? Many people think that this is an impossible question to answer, and I think Elijah was very brave to tackle it!

Key: The evidence is in the actual Bible passage itself.

Firstly, we have to look at the background to this situation.

King Ahab was married to Jezebel. She worshipped a false god called Baal and got Ahab to worship him too. That was a bad mistake because Ahab was king of the Israelites, God's people, and God was very angry that the king was not worshipping Him. The Bible tells us He is a jealous God. You might think that is strange but God has emotions just like us. He created us after all and we are made in His image. A long time before, God had made the nation of Israel to be His people and to serve Him only. He didn't want them to go after other gods.

In those days there was a prophet called Elijah and God told him to speak to Ahab. There had been no rain for three years and Ahab blamed Elijah. He even called him a "troublemaker"! Now Elijah was brave and answered the king back. "No," he said, "there's been no rain because you don't obey God." Then Elijah said that he could prove that God was real, and Baal was not, and Ahab agreed to a contest on Mount Carmel. Elijah wasn't just doing this to prove a point to Ahab, he was also showing the Israelites who they should worship because many of them served Baal too.

On the day, there were 450 false prophets of Baal and they built a big altar, killed a bull ready for the sacrifice, and prayed to Baal to set it all on fire. The prophets shouted and danced and asked their god to bring the fire.

But nothing happened.

Elijah started to taunt them. "Where is your god?" he asked. "Is he sleeping or travelling?" Some versions even say, "Is your god on the toilet?"! So the prophets shouted and danced even louder and cut themselves in the effort to get their god to answer.

But still nothing happened.

Fascinating Fact:
When people call someone a Jezebel they mean they are evil and deceitful. They are scheming and plotting against others.

When they were exhausted, Elijah took twelve stones (one for each of the twelve tribes of Israel) and built an altar with them. After that he piled on wood and killed his bull and put his sacrifice on top. Then he did something incredible – he poured water on it! Not just a little, he soaked it all. The crowd were shocked. How could God set it on fire now?

All eyes on him, Elijah prayed to the God of Israel. He asked Him to show the people that He was their God and that this event would turn their hearts back to Him.

As everyone stood transfixed, watching the altar, fire came down from heaven. It burnt everything: the bull, the wood, the stones and even the dust of the ground. Now the people knew that God was real! They turned back to God and said sorry to Him. Then Elijah commanded all the false prophets be put to death so they couldn't mislead the people anymore. Shortly afterwards God sent rain again, which ended the drought.

This is an amazing account for several reasons: one, it shows how Elijah trusted God; two, that God is powerful and evil is no match for Him; and three, He is real. Sometimes God shows us He is there, but most of the time He wants us to trust that He is real, even when we can't see Him, and that's called faith.

Gem: We must remember that God is real even when other people tell us He isn't. We know He is real because of the Bible, our own experiences and other people's testimonies.

Fascinating Fact:

Baal was a fertility god and people even sacrificed their children to him. He was the god of the Canaanites, who were the people who lived in the land before the Israelites took it over. God had warned His people not to worship Baal, but they did anyway.

Why did the widow keep on knocking?

Luke 18:1–5:

Then Jesus told his disciples a parable to show them that they should always pray and not give up. He said: "In a certain town there was a judge who neither feared God nor cared what people thought. And there was a widow in that town who kept coming to him with the plea, 'Grant me justice against my adversary.'

"For some time he refused. But finally he said to himself, 'Even though I don't fear God or care what people think, yet because this widow keeps bothering me, I will see that she gets justice, so that she won't eventually come and attack me!'"

I remember reading this passage and thinking, why is Jesus talking about a grumpy judge and a widow who just won't go away, and what has that got to do with me?

Key: This is answered in the first verse – it was a story to show the disciples to pray and not give up.

This story is actually quite funny. I truly believe God has a good sense of humour! Firstly, you have a mean judge who doesn't care about

anything but himself while we know that judges are meant to be fair and want the best for us. Then Jesus tells us about a widow who comes to the judge for justice – that means she wants to have respect from him and be treated fairly. She obviously feels that her adversary (her enemy) has treated her badly and goes to the only person who can help her. When he doesn't do what she expected, instead of giving up, she goes back again and again until he gives her what she wants because he thinks he might be attacked by her!

Like the widow we have to be persistent in our prayers – that means we need to keep going back to God again and again and not give up. Sometimes it feels as if our prayers are hitting the ceiling and not reaching Him, and that can make us think He hasn't heard us. But God is not an unfair, mean judge. He is loving and caring and will give up what is right for us at the right time. The widow didn't keep on because she wanted her own way, it was because she knew what was right and just.

The Bible tells us clearly that God knows what we are going to pray even before we say it.

Matthew 6:8:

Do not be like them, for your Father knows what you need before you ask him.

So that means we have to have faith; faith that God hears us, even when we are not sure. Doubt has a habit of creeping in, and Jesus is saying, "Don't let it get to you. Your answer might be just around the corner, so don't give in." Keep on praying and keep on trusting Him.

Gem: We need to keep on praying even when we don't receive an answer from God straight away.

Fascinating Fact:

Christians often say "Amen" at the end of their prayers. "Amen" means "so be it" or "I agree". It can also be linked to trustworthiness and truth. So saying "Amen" lets God know we have said a prayer that we really mean from the heart. We can be assured that God has heard our prayer. Also, when we say it with others it means we agree with their prayer too.

How do we pray?

> **Matthew 6:7–8:**
>
> "And when you pray, do not keep on babbling like pagans, for they think they will be heard because of their many words. Do not be like them, for your Father knows what you need before you ask him."

When I first became a Christian I didn't know a lot about prayer. I'd always done my night-time prayers as a child and this carried on into my adult life but, other than that, I didn't pray a lot apart from some desperate prayers when I was stuck and needed God's help!

Key: Don't use too many words. God the Father knows what you need even before you ask.

Jesus went up onto a hillside and started to teach about the way God wanted people to live. His followers, the disciples, were there, as were a crowd of people who wanted to hear Him speak. Also there were the Pharisees, scribes and priests who all thought they were living the life God wanted them to, but Jesus knew that many of them did things to make themselves look good to others and He told them that would be their reward rather than an eternal one in heaven.

When Jesus said "don't babble on like the pagans" (or Gentiles – non-Jews) He was referring to those people who keep on praying, going over and over the same point as if God is deaf! The point He made here is incredible – God knows what we are going to say before we even say it!

So how do we pray? Jesus instructed those listening to say the Lord's Prayer, to be specific in what we pray and don't go on in a meaningless way. God is listening and will hear our prayers and He will answer them as He feels fit. You may ask, if God knows everything, then why do we have to pray at all? Well, that's because we have a relationship and that is part of it, communicating with Him. Can you imagine not talking to your mum or a family member when you need something? They probably know already but like to be asked – it's the same with God.

We read in **Matthew 6:9–13** that Jesus said, "This, then, is how you should pray…"

Our Father in heaven – we are addressing a real God, who is also our Father.

Hallowed be your name – we are acknowledging God as holy.

Your kingdom come, your will be done, on earth as it is in heaven – God has a kingdom and we are asking Him to do on earth what He is already doing in heaven.

Give us today our daily bread – we trust God every day for what we need.

And forgive us our debts, as we also have forgiven our debtors – we must forgive others because God has forgiven us.

And lead us not into temptation – help us not to do bad things.

But deliver us from the evil one – keep us from the devil and his evil schemes.

This is a guide for us on how to pray, not in a meaningless way, but to let Him know what we need now. Though it isn't always about what we want, sometimes we may just want to thank Him and praise Him for who He is. We can go somewhere quiet, talk to God just as we would a good friend and trust that He will do what is right for us at the right time.

Fascinating Fact:
Jesus prayed a lot! It is recorded that He prayed at least 25 times in the New Testament, though I'm sure there were a lot more times when He prayed that weren't written down. He often went somewhere on His own and called God His Father, Abba, which is a bit like our word Daddy.

Gem: God is good and He will hear our prayers, and act on them, if we pray with the right motive. It can help us develop our relationship with Him.

> Our Father in heaven. Hallowed be your name. Your kingdom come, your will be done on earth as it is in heaven…

Does God do bad things?

Matthew 7:9–11:

"Which of you, if your son asks for bread, will give him a stone? Or if he asks for a fish, will give him a snake? If you, then, though you are evil, know how to give good gifts to your children, how much more will your Father in heaven give good gifts to those who ask him!"

Key: We must get to know the character of God and understand that He loves us and doesn't want to harm us.

What is Jesus on about? What dad would give his son or daughter a stone or snake? It sounds bizarre! And why is Jesus calling people evil? We have to look at the passage in detail.

When Jesus calls us evil, He doesn't mean that we are out and out wicked but that we are sinful. From the time we are born we sin. We do wrong things and that is part of our nature. Even when we give our lives to Jesus we can still do bad things. Jesus is saying that even though we are sinners we still know how to treat our children right. If they say, "Please can we have some nice food?" we wouldn't think of giving them something awful like a stone or a snake! Now God is Jesus's Father and He is our Father too. So if we pray to Him and ask Him for something good, we can expect Him to give us something good, not bad, because He is more loving and holy than our earthly parents.

So what we see in this passage is that God is our Father, that He is kind and loving and, above all, wants the best for us. He will never do anything to hurt us or be cruel to us. This is important to understand because so many people think that when bad things happen to them it is God's fault, but it isn't. He is a God of love.

Interestingly, the two examples in this passage are found in other parts of the Bible too. In **Matthew 4** Jesus was in the desert and had not eaten for 40 days and was hungry, when the devil came and said he could turn the stones into bread. In **Genesis 3** the devil is shown as a serpent, which is a snake.

I'm sure it wasn't a coincidence that Jesus chose these two items to use in His illustration.

Some people may say, "Hang on a minute, what about Job?" Job was a man in the Old Testament who had an horrendous time. He was a good man who did good things and had it all: wife, children, animals, riches and respect. Then in one day he loses all his children and his wealth. Later he was covered in boils. They were so bad that he had to scrape his skin with shards of pottery. Ouch!

Why did this happen to him? It wasn't because of anything Job had done but because the devil asked God if he could see if he could get Job to curse God. He wanted to see if Job loved God for Himself or because of all the things he had on earth. He had thrown the gauntlet down, and God accepted.

Through all the trials Job stuck with God and, in the end, he was rewarded with more children and wealth. The question is, did God allow this because He didn't love Job? No, He did it because He knew that Job was a righteous man and He knew he had faith. Amazingly, Job trusted God, and God trusted Job.

Job says in the middle of his trial in **Job 13:15**:

"Though he slay me, yet will I hope in him."

We see in **Psalm 100:5**:

For the Lord is good and his love endures for ever.

So we can see that we are in a spiritual battle and if we trust God we will come out with a stronger faith and we will get to know God better. God is good and He is love, and He only wants what is best for us. As shown with Job, it was not God who did bad things to him but the devil. What he means for evil God can, and does, use for good. God gives us good gifts and we can trust Him to do that.

Gem: We must always remember that God is good, and that He is love. He wants the best for us and wants us to love Him in return. We can always trust Him to do the right thing.

Fascinating Fact:

The word "gift" can be many things. Gifts can be presents, as in your birthday or Christmas presents. It can be your talents or your personality, such as I can play tennis really well or you can make others laugh. It can also mean the gift of something precious, like a child. We can say someone is God's gift to us, meaning they have been kind to us. We can say that Jesus is the ultimate gift to us from God.

Should the elder son have been so jealous of his brother?

Luke 15:25–30:

"Meanwhile, the elder son was in the field. When he came near the house, he heard music and dancing. So he called one of the servants and asked him what was going on. 'Your brother has come,' he replied, 'and your father has killed the fattened calf because he has him back safe and sound.'

"The elder brother became angry and refused to go in. So his father went out and pleaded with him. But he answered his father, 'Look! All these years I've been slaving for you and never disobeyed your orders. Yet you never gave me even a young goat so I could celebrate with my friends. But when this son of yours who has squandered your property with prostitutes comes home, you kill the fattened calf for him!'"

Wow, you can just feel his anger! He's so angry and, it feels, rightly so. His younger brother disappeared with his half of the inheritance, wasted it, and then came home to a party, while he was at home doing the right thing. I can see his point, and would have felt the same if I had been him. But was he right?

Key: Look at how each character is behaving and why. Remember how God wants us to act.

Let's see what each character does…

The younger son: he asks his dad for his share of the inheritance money – an awful thing to do. It's like saying, "I can't wait for you to die, so I'll have my money now." Then he takes the money and wastes it on wild and reckless living and then eventually, when he has nothing left, he comes home. He's really sorry and doesn't even expect his dad to take him back as his son, just as a servant. He knows that what he has done is wrong.

The elder son: he's dutiful, staying home with his dad and looking after the farm. He doesn't seem to miss his younger brother, and when he returns he is jealous, not pleased, that he's come home.

The father: he feels sad that his youngest son wanted the money, but he gave it to him anyway. When his son comes back he is over the moon. He has been waiting for him – we know that because he runs to him even before he gets to the house – and throws a huge party. He thought his son had died and he would never see him again and is thrilled to have him home safely.

So when we break it down like that, it's not quite what we first thought. What the younger son did was wrong, but when he came back he was very sorry and was just grateful to be home. The father was amazing! He should have been angry but no, he loved his son so much, he

wanted to celebrate his return with everyone around him, and that included his other son. A family reunion.

So can you imagine his sorrow when he finds his elder son, thinking he would be overjoyed at the return of his brother, full of anger and jealousy. It must have broken his heart. The father would have given his elder son anything he wanted if he had asked, but he never did. We don't know what happened next, but my guess is he sulked and didn't enjoy the party, sitting outside while wonderful things were happening inside.

Sadly, both sons didn't have the right relationship with their father. They were both lost. The younger son was rebellious and the elder son didn't appreciate what he had all around him, and this can happen to us too. We can become self-righteous and think we have earned our place with God, but in reality we can't do that. We have to become like the younger son, realising that we have made mistakes and saying sorry to God for what we've done, and not wanting to do it again. We need to humble ourselves and know that only God is good and holy. It's only by God's grace, which we cannot earn but He gives to us freely, that we can get close to Him.

One day there will be a big party in heaven and only those who know God will be allowed to go in. There will be many outside who think they should be able to join in, but will be told no. The Bible says:

Ephesians 2:8–9:

For it is by grace you have been saved, through faith – and this is not of yourselves, it is the gift of God – not by works, so that no one may boast.

Gem: We can't earn our way to God but only through repentance – which means turning away from our sin and saying sorry for the wrong things we have done.

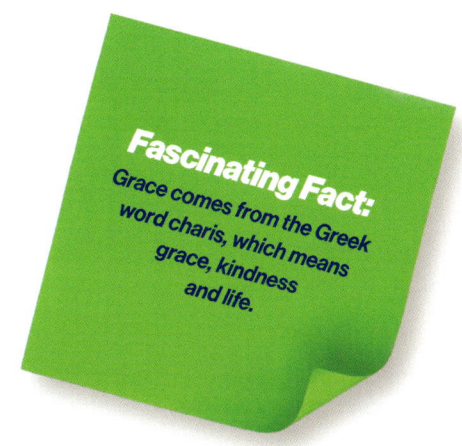

Fascinating Fact: Grace comes from the Greek word charis, which means grace, kindness and life.

Did the sun really stand still and the moon stop moving?

Joshua 10:12–14:

On the day the LORD gave the Amorites over to Israel, Joshua said to the LORD in the presence of Israel: "Sun, stand still over Gibeon, and you, moon, over the Valley of Aijalon." So the sun stood still, and the moon stopped, till the nation avenged itself on its enemies, as it is written in the Book of Jashar.

The sun stopped in the middle of the sky and delayed going down about a full day. There has never been a day like it before or since, a day when the LORD listened to a human being. Surely the LORD was fighting for Israel!

This Bible passage really fascinates me – can you imagine the sun standing still and the moon not moving in the sky? It sounds incredible!

Key: God is the creator of the sun and moon. Also look at similar Bible passages.

Let us look at what is happening here. Joshua is leading the Israelites in battle to fight their enemies. In the middle of the battle God sends down huge hailstones that kill quite of few of them. Then Joshua asks the Lord to make the sun stand still and the moon to stop moving ... and He does! Then Joshua and the Israelites defeat the rest of their enemies.

So why does Joshua ask for this miracle to happen? It is most likely that they wanted the extra light to keep fighting as they had the upper hand, or it might be they needed more time. They were fighting for the land that God had promised to them. He had commanded them to clear out all of the people who lived there and that is what they were doing. That might seem harsh to us, but it was because they were doing wicked things and God didn't want the Israelites mixing with them.

We may not be able to explain this with science and sometimes we just have to trust that God can do it. If we believe He is the creator then He

Fascinating Fact:
The largest hailstone in recent times was 8 inches across (22cm), which is the size of a football!

can do what He wants with His creation! There was another time where God did something amazing with the sun. It was in **2 Kings 20:9–11**:

Isaiah answered, "This is the Lord's sign to you that the Lord will do what he has promised: shall the shadow go forward ten steps, or shall it go back ten steps?"

"It is a simple matter for the shadow to go forward ten steps," said Hezekiah. "Rather, let it go back ten steps."

Then the prophet Isaiah called on the Lord, and the Lord made the shadow go back the ten steps it had gone down on the stairway of Ahaz.

This meant that the sun went backwards! How incredible is that? The Bible tells us that nothing is impossible for God.

For Joshua to ask God to do this miracle he must have had a lot of faith in Him. He knew in his heart that God could do it and He also knew that God was on the side of the Israelites, so that would have increased his confidence. God had spoken to him and he trusted Him.

Joshua 10:8:

The LORD said to Joshua, "Do not be afraid of them; I have given them into your hand. Not one of them will be able to withstand you."

Also, the pagan people in the land of Canaan worshipped the sun and moon, so God could have been showing them that He was higher than these celestial bodies.

Another example that God showed He was more powerful than the false gods that the pagans worshipped was in **1 Samuel 5:1–3**:

After the Philistines had captured the ark of God, they took it from Ebenezer to Ashdod. Then they carried the ark into Dagon's temple and set it beside Dagon. When the people of Ashdod rose early the next day, there was Dagon, fallen on his face on the ground before the ark of the LORD!

God didn't need to prove Himself to anyone but He wasn't going to be mocked either. In the Ten Commandments we are told that He is to be worshipped above everything else.

Exodus 20:3:

You shall have no other gods before me.

Gem: We must put God first in our lives before any other thing. That includes computer games and celebrities! He is in control of everything in and around the earth.

Fascinating Fact:

The god Dagon was known as the fish-god, as he was half man and had the tail of a fish. A sort of merman – the male version of a mermaid. He was worshipped by the Philistines, the enemies of the Israelites. He was a false god, and a demonic spirit.

Why did the prophets do weird things?

Isaiah 20:1–2:

In the year that the supreme commander, sent by Sargon king of Assyria, came to Ashdod and attacked and captured it – at that time the Lord spoke through Isaiah son of Amoz. He said to him, "Take off the sackcloth from your body and the sandals from your feet." And he did so, going around stripped and barefoot.

Jeremiah 13:3–5:

Then the word of the Lord came to me a second time: "Take the belt you bought and are wearing around your waist, and go now to Perath and hide it there in a crevice in the rocks." So I went and hid it at Perath, as the Lord told me.

Jeremiah 27:1–2:

Early in the reign of Zedekiah, son of Josiah king of Judah, this word came to Jeremiah from the Lord: this is what the Lord said to me: "Make a yoke out of straps and crossbars and put it on your neck."

Ezekiel 3:3:

Then he said to me, "Son of man, eat this scroll I am giving you and fill your stomach with it." So I ate it, and it tasted as sweet as honey in my mouth.

Hosea 1:6:

Then the Lord said to Hosea, "Call her Lo-Ruhamah (which means 'not loved'), for I will no longer show love to Israel, that I should at all forgive them."

Hosea 1:9:

Then the Lord said, "Call him Lo-Ammi (which means 'not my people'), for you are not my people and I am not your God."

These are just some of the strange things the prophets did in the Old Testament. We've already seen that Balaam had a donkey talk to him and God used some unusual tactics to get His message through. But why would God get His prophets to do odd things? Some of it is very humiliating!

Key: These passages talk about God and His people Israel, and how He feels about them and what they are doing.

Fascinating Fact:

The first yokes were used around 4,000 BC. In the Bible the yoke is often talked about as being under the rule of another country. It can also mean that you are yoked to someone and that you work together for a common purpose.

Looking at the above passages we can see that Isaiah walked around naked and barefoot. Jeremiah put his belt in a crack in a rock – some versions say his "undergarment" – his underpants! Ezekiel ate a scroll and it tasted sweet, and Hosea had to call his children strange names. In the New Testament Jesus talked in parables – stories with meanings – and in the Old Testament God talked to His people Israel by His prophets. They were men who heard from God and told the message to Israel. Now I don't know about you but I would have really struggled with doing some of these!

Let's have a quick look at what was going on around the time of these prophets. Israel had divided in two: Israel and Judah. Often, they were ruled by bad kings who did terrible things and wanted power and riches, rather than listen to what God wanted to do. So the prophets were sent to illustrate God's plan for them at that time and sometimes for the nations around them. So what were they doing in these situations?

Isaiah went around naked because God was saying to Egypt and Cush that they would go into captivity shamed and naked. Israel had looked to Egypt for their protection instead of looking to God and so He took them away. He wanted Israel to look only to Him for help.

When Jeremiah was eventually told to go and get his belt it was completely ruined and of no use. God told him to tell Judah that they will be like the belt, of no use at all, because of their stubborn hearts, refusing to follow God.

Can you imagine wearing a heavy wooden yoke on your shoulders? No, me neither! Now a yoke is a wooden bar that went across two oxen so that they could plough the field together. Jeremiah made one as God had described, put it on and told Judah it was because they must come under the yoke of the king of Babylon. If they served him and his people, God would let them live.

Ezekiel takes a scroll from God and eats it and it tastes sweet. This is because the Word of God is good, but the message wasn't. Ezekiel had to tell Judah that there were more bad things coming to them. They had already been taken away to live in a foreign land because they disobeyed God. They were hard-hearted and had turned away from God.

So was the scroll a real scroll? My thinking is it probably wasn't, more that God wanted Ezekiel to have His Word in his spirit and God sort of

downloaded it into him in a vision so that he could give God's message to the Israelites.

Last, but not least, we have Hosea. Now he didn't get off any lighter than the other prophets. He had to marry a woman who would go and run off with other men! And to top it all off he had to call his children very sad names. This was to show – literally – to Israel that God was fed up with them worshipping other gods and ignoring Him. You would think they would learn their lesson at some point!

So there we are. What looked to us like mad men, were actually faithful men who loved God and were willing to obey Him and do what He asked them to do, however crazy it seemed. God knew that a picture or an example would enable the Israelites to understand His message better. Today God can and does ask us to do things for Him and, just like prophets, He will give us His Spirit to accomplish the task.

Gem: It is important to love God with your whole heart and to listen to Him. Disobeying Him will cause you to go down the wrong path and end up in a bad place. But if we are faithful, He will bless us and we will have the best friend ever.

Should Jesus have been angry at the temple sellers?

Matthew 21:12–13:

Jesus entered the temple courts and drove out all who were buying and selling there. He overturned the tables of the money-changers and the benches of those selling doves. "It is written," he said to them, "'My house will be called a house of prayer,' but you are making it a 'den of robbers.'"

In **Matthew 11:29** it says:

Take my yoke upon you and learn from me, for I am gentle and humble in heart, and you will find rest for your souls.

This is Jesus speaking and we often feel that He was mild mannered, but Matthew 21 shows us a different side to Him. It's a dramatic scene and no one there would have described Him as gentle and mild. So why did Jesus get angry? Doesn't the Bible say we should have self-control?

Key: Look at the fruits of the Holy Spirit, other verses about anger and Jesus's character.

The main thing here is this: if Jesus was allowed to be angry, then we can too! Does this give us permission to have a go at people and not think we are sinning? Let's have a look at what the Bible tells us about anger:

Ephesians 4:26–27:

"In your anger do not sin": do not let the sun go down while you are still angry, and do not give the devil a foothold.

James 1:19:

My dear brothers and sisters, take note of this: everyone should be quick to listen, slow to speak and slow to become angry.

There are many other verses about anger, but it looks pretty clear that we should be slow to anger, and not to sin if we do become angry. As we saw in the "Bit and the Rudder" we have the fruit of the Holy Spirit to help us. To remind us, they are:

Love, Joy, Peace, Forbearance, Kindness, Goodness, Faithfulness, Gentleness, Self-control.

Displaying these fruit in our daily lives is how God wants us to be. We can only do this with the help of the Holy Spirit and, even then, we sometimes fail! They are good actions and they produce good fruit (results). We know that Jesus was full of the Holy Spirit and therefore He would live by these fruit. We also know that Jesus was sinless, and so couldn't sin. So how did He get angry and not sin?

I think the key verse is when it says you can get angry but do not sin, and that means that if we do sin we give the devil a foothold. So Jesus was angry at the temple sellers for good reason. They were there cheating people – we know that because it says "a den of robbers" – and the focus of the temple should have been prayer, but people weren't focused on prayer and God but on money. What Jesus was experiencing was righteous anger, which is anger that is directed to others because they are not respecting God. God is to be worshipped above everything else and these men worshipped money, not God. They were also leading the people who came to worship in the temple away from God by making it about them and what they wanted.

Fascinating Fact: Solomon built the first temple on Mount Moriah, now known as the Temple Mount in Jerusalem.

We learn from the Old Testament that God got angry when the Israelites (His chosen people) left Him and went off with other false gods.

So what does this all mean for us and our anger? How can we live better?

We must be slow to get angry. In other words, don't fly off the handle! We must be sure that our anger is righteous and not for our own gain.

We must remember that we are representing God and people look to us and see what our Christian faith means to us. If we are always getting angry and hurting others, then we will not be a good representative for Him.

Lastly, when Jesus had thrown out the temple sellers, the lame and blind came in and were healed. They went away happy but the chief priests and teachers of the Law were not. That's because their hearts were hard and they couldn't see that Jesus was from God.

Gem: We must be slow to anger, and when we do get angry we must be sure it is for God and not for us. It is important to have our hearts set on God and not on money.

Why did the man with one talent get it taken away?

Matthew 25:14–18, 24–28:

Again, it will be like a man going on a journey, who called his servants and entrusted his wealth to them. To one he gave five bags of gold, to another two bags, and to another one bag, each according to his ability. Then he went on his journey. The man who had received five bags of gold went at once and put his money to work and gained five bags more. So also, the one with two bags of gold gained two more. But the man who had received one bag went off, dug a hole in the ground and hid his master's money . . .

Then the man who had received one bag of gold came. "Master," he said, "I knew that you are a hard man, harvesting where you have not sown and gathering where you have not scattered seed. So I was afraid and went out and hid your gold in the ground. See, here is what belongs to you." His master replied, "You wicked, lazy servant! So you knew that I harvest where I have not sown and gather where I have not scattered seed? Well then, you should have put my money on deposit with the bankers, so that when I returned I would have received it back with interest. So take the bag of gold from him and give it to the one who has ten bags."

I remember reading this and thinking that is really harsh! I mean, the man didn't invest the money but he did keep it safe. I thought that the master's reaction was very cruel.

Key: The servant with one bag of gold was afraid of his master and instead of doing what he was asked to do, he buried it in fear. The other key is that the master entrusted them with his wealth.

Let's look at the scenario. Jesus is telling His followers a parable about a man who had three servants and he gave them different amounts

of gold to look after while he was gone. He wanted them to invest it so that when he came back he would have his wealth increased. When the man arrived back from his trip he found that the first man who had five bags had five more, the man with two had two more and the last servant had nothing extra, just the one bag that he was given.

So why was Jesus telling this story and what can we learn from it? Jesus knew that He would go to heaven after His death and resurrection and leave the work of His kingdom to everyone who follows Him.

How can we do this work?

Well, we all have our own gifts and talents and He wants us to use them to build His kingdom. We may be good at making friends, or being kind to the poor, or excel at crafts, maths or sport. Whatever we have we can use it to help people come to know Jesus.

One day Jesus will return to the earth and He will find out just how we have lived our lives for Him. That's a scary thought!

So, back to the parable. The master entrusted his money to his servants. Now that's a big deal. Would you give all your money to someone to look after? "Entrusted" means to trust, so he must have had a good relationship with his servants to do that. He gave clear instructions for them so they knew what they had to do.

For the two that had increased his wealth we read in **Matthew 25:23** that he said:

"Well done good and faithful servant! You have been faithful with a few things; I will put you in charge of many things. Come and share your master's happiness!"

The news in verse 29 wasn't so good for the servant who had hidden his bag.

"Whoever does not have, even what they have will be taken from them."

At first this does seem harsh, but if you look closer you will see that it was done in fairness. We can see that the master knew his servants well. The first two servants had a good enough relationship with their master and so they:

Knew the master trusted them enough to risk his money.

Were willing to step out in faith to please him.

Now look at the last servant. It didn't seem that he had a good relationship with the master as he was afraid of him and he had a stinking attitude! Look at what he says on his master's return. Instead of greeting him, he says rudely, "I knew you were a hard man." He didn't do what was asked of him and he seemed to be a lazy man, who couldn't be bothered to do anything. It would have taken some effort to get more money but he wasn't willing to put any in. Despite knowing this man, and his appalling attitude, the master still gave him a chance, and that says love and kindness to me.

Jesus is telling us that just like the master in the parable, although He has gone away, He will return one day. When He does He wants to find us working for His kingdom, building it up with the gifts and talents that He has given us.

Gem: We must have a good relationship with God, keep a good attitude and seek to serve Him in all we do and to put effort into building His kingdom.

Fascinating Fact:

The chemical symbol of gold is Au, which comes from the Latin name for gold, aurum, meaning "glowing dawn". If you've seen a sunrise you will see how apt this name is.

COMPLICATED CONCEPTS

Why did Jesus say, "Eat Me"?

John 6:47–51:

"Very truly I tell you, the one who believes has eternal life. I am the bread of life. Your ancestors ate the manna in the wilderness, yet they died. But here is the bread that comes down from heaven, which anyone may eat and not die. I am the living bread that came down from heaven. Whoever eats this bread will live forever. This bread is my flesh, which I will give for the life of the world."

This is just freaky! In fact I don't think there is any other passage in the Bible as freaky as this one! How can Jesus become bread? When Jesus said this, the people thought he was mad.

Key: Jesus said, "I am living bread from heaven and you can live forever if you eat it." Also look at the verses before this one and in the Old Testament on the theme of bread, especially Exodus 16:4 and Exodus 25:30.

I must admit, if I was there at the time I'd probably have said the same thing. It's a hard thing to get your head round. To get a better understanding, we have to look at the verses before and we see that Jesus had fed them. When he started talking to the people again, they asked for a sign that He was who He said He was and they mentioned the manna. Jesus cleverly links these two things to the topic of eternal life.

The manna: when the Israelites were living in the desert they ran out of food so God sent them bread from heaven to keep them alive. It was called manna and was a white wafer that tasted like coriander.

Feeding the 5,000: just before this conversation with the people, Jesus had fed the 5,000 with bread and fish. They were hungry but instead of sending them away, He fed them.

In the days when Jesus lived, people depended on bread to survive as there were no supermarkets in those days and they made it daily. The people Jesus was speaking to, the Jews, had a history of being with God and knew Him from far away but they didn't know Him personally. Jesus was telling them that if they ate His bread they would have eternal life. We read in **John 6** that He said to them:

"The bread of God is the bread that comes down from heaven and gives life to the world."

He says that He will never turn away the people who come to Him and that He came from heaven.

Many of them said:
"How can this man give us his flesh to eat?"

Jesus replied to them:
"Very truly I tell you, unless you eat the flesh of the Son of Man and drink his blood, you have no life in you. Whoever eats my flesh and drinks my blood has eternal life, and I will raise them up at the last day."

Fascinating Fact:
In medieval times stale bread was used as a plate called a trencher. After it was used it was given to the poor to eat.

So how do we understand what Jesus is saying? We have to divide it up into two sections:

The real, physical world

The spiritual world

In the real world, Jesus knew that people needed to eat to stay alive and so He fed them with real food. In the spiritual world, He knows that they will die and face an eternity without God so He gives them spiritual food. And we can only be with God forever if we have faith in Jesus, which is why He says, "Eat this bread." We are not to "eat" Jesus but to believe in Him and follow Him; we can only be truly satisfied if we have Him in our lives.

> **Fascinating Fact:**
> When Jesus died on the cross the curtain in the temple (which kept God separate from the people) ripped in two, from top to bottom. Usually people would tear material from the bottom to the top. This was a sign to show the people that they could now have access to Him directly.

There is also another point to what Jesus is saying. At the last supper He talked about the bread and the wine.

Matthew 26:26:

While they were eating, Jesus took bread, and when he had given thanks, he broke it and gave it to his disciples, saying, "Take and eat; this is my body."

This was just before He was crucified and He was telling His disciples that this was a new covenant (an agreement between man and God) whereby the people didn't need to go to a priest but could have direct communication to God through Jesus. Before Jesus died, people had to go to the priest and give offerings of animals as a sacrifice for their sins. After Jesus had been resurrected there was no need for sacrifice anymore because He had become the final sacrifice. When we believe in Jesus and know that He has died for our sins, it takes away the barrier between us and God. Incredible, eh?

Gem: We can trust God to feed us in this life and He will provide us with the spiritual nourishment we need to grow in faith and one day be with Him in heaven.

Does Jesus really want us to cut off our hand?

Matthew 5:29–30:

"If your right eye causes you to stumble, gouge it out and throw it away. It is better for you to lose one part of your body than for your whole body to be thrown into hell. And if your right hand causes you to stumble, cut it off and throw it away. It is better for you to lose one part of your body than for your whole body to go into hell."

Seriously?! We know that Jesus said some radical things, but surely He wouldn't want us to do anything as gory as this? I think we should take a closer look and see the real meaning of this puzzling passage...

Key: Sometimes we have to "read between the lines" of what Jesus is saying.

The first thing we need to look at is the point Jesus is making. He says: "It is better for you to lose one part of your body than for your whole body to be thrown into hell."

Ok, so that's pretty clear. Jesus is saying that hell is a real place and He doesn't want us to go there. Jesus talks quite a bit about hell in the Bible and says it's a place where we would be separated from God. A place where there is "gnashing of teeth", darkness and eternal torment and fire. You can see why He wants no-one to go there!

The Bible also tells us in **John 3:16**:

For God so loved the world that he gave his one and only Son, that whoever believes in him shall not perish but have eternal life.

God the Father, God the Son and God the Holy Spirit want us to spend eternity with them. They do not want us to have eternity away from them and all that entails, so it makes sense that Jesus – God on earth – would warn us. If I had a child near an open fire I would keep them away from it and tell them they could be badly hurt if they touched it. Imagine, though, that the child decided to go too close to the fire and was in danger. I wouldn't just say, "Ah, don't go near the fire." No, I would shout, "Stop! Don't touch!" So in effect, that is what Jesus is doing here. He's not saying in a soft way, "Hell is awful so don't go there." No, He is saying, "Stop! Think what you are doing. If your behaviour is taking you on the broad path to destruction, don't do it." And to drive the point home He is using language that is striking. We call it hyperbole. An example would be, "I'm so hungry I could eat a horse." Now we wouldn't really eat a horse, would we?!

Fascinating Fact:
The Bible says in Isaiah that God has us engraved on His hands and He will never forget us. What a comforting thought.

So no, we don't really need to gouge out an eye or cut off a hand. We do, however, need to check our behaviour and see that what we are doing is not taking us on the wrong path. The Bible makes it clear there is a narrow way to life and a broad way to destruction.

The interesting thing is that these verses follow a passage about adultery. He warns married men not to look at a woman with lust, otherwise they have already committed adultery in their heart. (This means he should stay faithful to his wife, and it also means women should be faithful too!) So it makes sense that He is talking about eyes and then He mentions the hand too, as another example.

So, we should be careful not to sin. Sin takes us away from God and it can start in a very small way, with just a look or a seemingly harmless action. We always have to be on our guard. The Bible tells us in **Proverbs 4:23**:

Above all else, guard your heart, for everything you do flows from it.

This means that we must protect our hearts against evil. For example, if we want to play a particular game, which we know might make us angry or want to fight, then we shouldn't play it. If we want to go somewhere or see someone who will make us make wrong choices, then we should not do it. We need to fix our eyes on Jesus.

Gem: We must be careful about what we see and hear and do. We can ask God to help us resist temptation by praying to Him.

Fascinating Fact:
Your eyes are so complex that they have more than two million working parts.

What does the number 666 stand for?

Revelation 13:16–18:

It also forced all people, great and small, rich and poor, free and slave, to receive a mark on their right hands or on their foreheads, so that they could not buy or sell unless they had the mark, which is the name of the beast or the number of its name.

This calls for wisdom. Let the person who has insight calculate the number of the beast, for it is the number of a man. That number is 666.

This passage comes from the book of Revelation, which is the last book of the Bible. Written by John (believed to be John, one of Jesus's disciples), it is full of mystery and symbols and can be quite exciting but also very confusing!

Key: Nobody could buy or sell without the beast's mark. It is the number of a man.

The number 666 crops up all over the place: in music, films, books, and it is often linked with the devil. This is because in Revelation it tells us about an evil trinity to match God's good trinity. (The devil copies God because he wants to be God.)

Good	**Evil**
God	Satan
Jesus	Antichrist (the beast)
Holy Spirit	False prophet

At some point in the future there will be a period when the devil (called the dragon in **Revelation 12:9**) will be allowed to reign on earth for a short time. He will do this through a man called the Antichrist (the beast) who will come and bring peace, but when he is in power he will set himself up against God and God's people. He will demand to be worshipped and no one will be able to buy or sell anything unless they have his mark, so people will have to make a choice to worship God or the Antichrist. The false prophet will do incredible signs and wonders to deceive people and be part of a global religion. Sounds a bit scary, doesn't it!

To understand what's going on we have to look back in time. You see it all boils down to worship. Satan doesn't like God being worshipped because he wants it all for himself. We saw this when he wanted Jesus to worship him in the desert:

Matthew 4:8–9:

Again, the devil took him to a very high mountain and showed him all the kingdoms of the world and their splendour. "All this I will give you," he said, "if you will bow down and worship me."

So who is Satan? In **Ezekiel 28:14** he was "the anointed cherub" and in **Ezekiel 28:12** he was "the seal of perfection, full of wisdom and perfect in beauty". That shows his importance in heaven and it went to his head. So he, and a third of the angels in heaven, fought God and His angels and lost the battle, and so Satan was thrown out of heaven.

Revelation 12:7–9:

Then war broke out in heaven, Michael and his angels fought against the dragon, and the dragon and his angels fought back. But he was not strong enough, and they lost their place in heaven. The great dragon was hurled down – that ancient snake called the devil, or Satan, who leads the whole world astray.

He didn't give up, though, and he's still trying to be top dog even now. This also explains why he doesn't like people who become Christians because they worship God. Though it will look like Satan has the upper hand, God will always be in ultimate control. In a lot of films we see fights between good and evil and this will be the ultimate fight between good and evil – God against Satan. At the very end the devil will end up in the lake of fire for all eternity.

> **Fascinating Fact:**
> Gematria is a Hebrew system where each letter has a number. Some famous people's names add up to 666 including the Roman emperor Nero, who persecuted Christians.

So back to 666. Reading our passage it says that people cannot buy or sell without the mark, and that is the name of the beast or the number of its name. In the Hebrew language each letter also has a number, for instance *aleph* is 1, *bet* is 2 and so on. This has led some people to calculate names that add up to 666. For instance Adolf Hitler's name adds up to 666. So the mark could represent ownership by someone with a name that adds up to 666. In the Bible numbers have meaning, so 6 is unholy or imperfect, like mankind, and 7 is holy or perfect, like God. So 666 could mean something unholy or imperfect, like the evil trinity or a man who falls short of God's perfection. Solomon received 666 talents of gold every year. This could indicate greed and a desire to have other things than God.

Fascinating Fact: The first Apple computer was priced at $666.

It is a mystery and no one really knows. The most important thing is to remember to follow God and not anyone else. If we have given our lives to Jesus then we are owned by Him. The Bible says that if we put God first then every thing else will come right.

Matthew 6:33:

But seek first his kingdom and his righteousness, and all these things will be given to you as well.

The most exciting thing is that one day Jesus will come back to earth to reign and the devil will not be able to do any harm to God's people anymore because he will be in the lake of fire!

Gem: We need God's wisdom to discern (understand) the signs of the times and we can ask Him for this. We also need to remember that the devil is already defeated by Jesus.

Should we really hate our parents?

> **Luke 14:25–27:**
>
> Large crowds were travelling with Jesus, and turning to them he said: "If anyone comes to me and does not hate father and mother, wife and children, brothers and sisters – yes, even their own life – such a person cannot be my disciple."

Seriously, does Jesus really mean hate our parents and family?! I remember the first time I read this passage and it got me very confused. Jesus, who tells us to love everyone, including our enemies, is telling us to hate the ones we love. It really looks like He is contradicting everything that God says, until we break it down.

Key: Look at a similar verse in a different gospel – Matthew 10:37. Also, don't forget Jesus's character, and what we read in other parts of the Bible, like the Ten Commandments.

Our first reaction is to think – what?! How can Jesus say such a thing? Then our minds start to question, well in that case, is the Bible real? That's exactly what the devil wants, to get us questioning the truth of it all. So we have to take a step back and look at it more objectively. We know that God doesn't lie so there must have been a reason for Jesus to use the word "hate".

The first thing we need to do is to look at a similar verse in **Matthew 10:37***:*

"Anyone who loves their father or mother more than me is not worthy of me."

It is saying the same thing but from a different viewpoint. It's a similar phrase but instead of hate it says if anyone "loves their father or mother *more* than me". Jesus is making a point here. Maybe He used the word "hate" because it would get people's attention or He may have been exaggerating it for effect. We don't really know, but we know certain things:

The Ten Commandments tell us that we must love our mothers and fathers.

Jesus tells us to love our neighbours as ourselves.

God is love.

We are to hate sin but not people.

So how do we explain what Jesus is saying? In both passages Jesus is saying, "Love Me more than anything else, even yourself." The Bible makes it clear that we are to put God first in our lives.

Matthew 6:33 says:

"But seek first his kingdom and his righteousness, and all these things will be given to you."

This verse comes from the chapter about worry – what shall we eat, drink, wear? God wants to be first and then He will look after us.

Jesus is driving the point home: don't follow after other things and put them first in your lives because God knows what is best for you. In fact, He is the perfect parent.

Gem: Put God first in your life and He will take care of everything else.

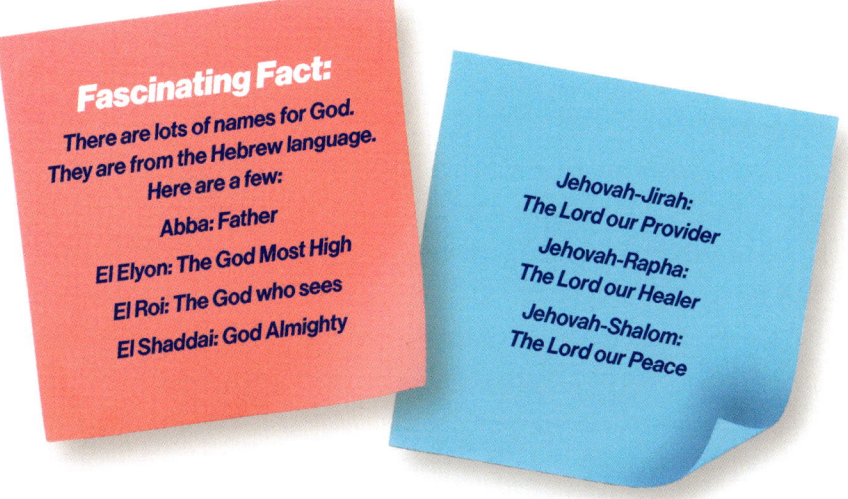

Fascinating Fact:
There are lots of names for God. They are from the Hebrew language. Here are a few:
Abba: Father
El Elyon: The God Most High
El Roi: The God who sees
El Shaddai: God Almighty

Jehovah-Jirah: The Lord our Provider
Jehovah-Rapha: The Lord our Healer
Jehovah-Shalom: The Lord our Peace

What does it mean to carry your cross?

> **Matthew 16:24–26 (ESV):**
>
> Then Jesus told his disciples, "If anyone would come after me, let him deny himself and take up his cross and follow me. For whoever would save his life will lose it, but whoever loses his life for my sake will find it. For what will it profit a man if he gains the whole world and forfeits his soul? Or what shall a man give in return for his soul?"

This was a huge puzzle to me for many years. I understood that Jesus was crucified on a cross for my sins, so that I didn't die in my sins and had eternal life, but why did I have to take up a cross and what does that actually mean?

Key: We must deny ourselves and follow Jesus.

God tends to work on us in stages. So firstly, I gave my heart to Jesus. Then I found a church and got baptised in water. I thought that was it, but no, it was only the beginning! There was another stage, and that was a bit scary for me. I'd been brought up in an Anglican church that was called "high church", with its incense, candles and solemn tradition. So when I went into a church where people were shouting "Hallelujah!" and waving their arms about, I wasn't sure if this was even about God! Thankfully, I hung on in there and, as I got used to it, I even started to raise my hands in praise to God too.

Then came the most amazing experience I had with the Holy Spirit. God knew He had to take me slowly or I would have freaked out! I went to a Full Gospel Business Men's meeting and they prayed for me to have the Holy Spirit. Well, I started to jump up and down and couldn't stop smiling, but something more important happened than God just filling me up with joy. The man at the front prayed over me and said, "Take up your cross and follow Jesus." I really had no idea what he was talking about, and it just left me feeling confused.

Over the years I kept wondering about that prayer. What did it mean? Where is my cross and how do I pick it up? So I went in search of an answer and here is what I discovered …

There is no physical cross to pick up. When Jesus died on the cross, He died for our sins. When we ask Jesus into our lives, we die to sin and our sinful ways. Now I know we will all still sin – no doubt about that!

So how do we die to our sins? Before people give their lives to Jesus they do what they like, when they like and only think of themselves. But when we say we will follow Jesus that means we will try and live like Him, but that isn't easy! We also have to live for others, so they will see Jesus in us. "Me?" you say. "How can I reflect Jesus?" We have to remember that whatever we do, even when we mess up, God can turn it to good. The Bible can help us here. When we read God's Word, we are able to apply it to our lives with the help of the Holy Spirit.

We often think of the cross in terms such as suffering and pain, because Jesus did suffer and was in pain on the cross. We don't have to go on a cross to be crucified but we do have a cross to bear. We may have to suffer for our faith. Sometimes we can be bullied because we won't deny Jesus or we have to miss out on something because it doesn't fit in with our belief.

Something we have to remember is that nothing is ever wasted. Our suffering is never in vain. It can help us grow in our faith, becoming stronger for Jesus. If everything went smoothly we would never have an opportunity to show others what our faith can do.

God has a plan! He always knows in advance what is going to happen to us and is never taken by surprise. That leads us onto my last point – we have to trust Jesus. He knows what is best for us and even when it seems to be so unfair or difficult, we have to trust that He knows the outcome.

2 Corinthians 12:9 (ESV):

But he said to me, "My grace is sufficient for you, for my power is made perfect in weakness."

Gem: To try and live like Jesus even in the hard times; trusting Him to give us strength for the moment.

Fascinating Fact:
In the first two centuries the Christians used a fish symbol and not a cross, which was thought to be a bit too gruesome. That would be like us wearing an electric chair today.

What did Jesus write on the ground?

John 8:3–11:

The teachers of the law and the Pharisees brought in a woman caught in adultery. They made her stand before the group and said to Jesus, "Teacher, this woman was caught in adultery. In the Law Moses commanded us to stone such women. Now what do you say?" They were using this question as a trap, in order to have a basis for accusing him.

But Jesus bent down and started to write on the ground with his finger. When they kept on questioning him, he straightened up and said to them, "Let any one of you who is without sin be the first to throw a stone at her." Again he stooped down and wrote on the ground. At this, those who heard began to go away one at a time, the older ones first, until only Jesus was left, with the woman still standing there. Jesus straightened up and asked her, "Woman, where are they? Has no one condemned you?"

"No one, sir," she said.

"Then neither do I condemn you," Jesus declared. "Go now and leave your life of sin."

This is a passage that really interested me as a young person. What did Jesus write on the ground? I was more taken with that question than the overall picture of a woman just about to be put to death. Call it curiosity, but I wanted to know!

Key: The clue here is that Jesus did not judge or condemn her. He makes the people with the stones see they are not sinless.

There is so much in this passage, and I don't just mean the amount of words! So let's divide it up and see . . .

Sin – what is sin? Sin is when we do wrong things. Because God is holy He can't be around sin, so it separates us from Him. Jesus doesn't say that the woman hasn't sinned; He tells her not to sin any more.

Adultery – this is when married people have other boyfriends or girlfriends. This can destroy relationships and goes against what the Bible says, that marriage is between one woman and one man. God says in the Ten Commandments for us to stay faithful to our husband or wife.

Pharisees – they were religious people who were in charge of the Temple and they told people what God expected of them. They wanted to get rid of Jesus because He was always upsetting them by doing things that they thought weren't right. In fact, He often told them what they were doing wrong. Because of this, they were always looking for ways to trap Him.

So what did Jesus write in the sand? Wow, I'd really like to have seen this! The Bible doesn't tell us and we can only guess. I wonder whether He was writing down a list of sins? Maybe even the Pharisees' sins. That would have really freaked them out!

Why did the Pharisees walk away and not stone the woman? Well, when Jesus said throw the stone if you haven't sinned, they all knew that they had done wrong and couldn't go through with their action. Also, there must have been something about the way Jesus was – He is God after all – that made them think, they knew He meant business!

Fascinating Fact:
There are three types of rock – igneous, sedimentary and metamorphic – and they are made from minerals. Did you know we even have rock in our toothpaste!

Jesus's love and compassion for the woman is shown in this tender scene. The woman who had faced certain death, was suddenly left all alone with Jesus. He was so kind and caring and treated her with dignity and respect. He didn't tell her off, just said go and sin no more. One thing we learn with Jesus, it's all about sin. Sin is the thing that puts a barrier between us and God, and that's why Jesus came: to remove that barrier and let us get close to God again.

Gem: Jesus didn't judge others and we must not judge others either. We all sin and restoring someone from sin is better than judging them.

Why did Jesus not condemn the shrewd manager?

Luke 16:1–8:

Jesus told his disciples: "There was a rich man whose manager was accused of wasting his possessions. So he called him in and asked him, 'What is this I hear about you? Give an account of your management, because you cannot be manager any longer.'

"The manager said to himself, 'What shall I do now? My master is taking away my job. I'm not strong enough to dig, and I'm ashamed to beg – I know what I'll do so that, when I lose my job here, people will welcome me into their houses.'

"So he called in each one of his master's debtors. He asked the first, 'How much do you owe my master?'

"'Three thousand litres of olive oil,' he replied.

"The manager told him, 'Take your bill, sit down quickly, and make it fifteen hundred.'

"Then he asked the second, 'And how much do you owe?'

"'Thirty tons of wheat,' he replied.

"He told him, 'Take your bill and make it twenty-four.'

"The master commended the dishonest manager because he had acted shrewdly."

This is a very odd parable that Jesus told His disciples. It used to puzzle me because the man was doing a bad thing, and yet Jesus praised him for it! How can that be right?

Key: We need to look at who Jesus was talking to and the verses that follow it.

Jesus told a lot of stories called parables, which are earthly stories with heavenly meanings. They were designed to let the people know what

He was talking about in an easy-to-understand way. It was usually linked with things they did everyday, such as farming and fishing. This particular parable was about money but it also had a deeper meaning.

Even though He was talking to His disciples, He knew the Pharisees were listening too. He knew that even though they looked like they loved God to other people, they really had hard hearts towards God and had other motives, like money.

In this parable the steward (that's someone who looks after something) gets caught out wasting his master's money, and his master says, "You're fired!"

So very cleverly the steward sets about making friends with the people who owe his master money, by making their bills smaller. He knows that when he has lost his job he will have friends who can help him out.

So what has this to do with us? The master actually said to the steward that he acted shrewdly. Now another word for shrewd is wise. So even though it

Fascinating Fact:
Paper money was first used in China over 1,000 years ago. It was called "flying money" because it could blow away in the wind.

was a bad thing that he did, it was a wise thing as it helped him in his time of need. Jesus is saying that if those people of the world can do wise things, then Christians can do the same; they can use their money and influence for good, to win others for His kingdom. He ends with a similar message to the man with the bags of gold – whoever is trusted with little can be trusted with much, and whoever is dishonest with little will also be dishonest with much. He says that if you cannot be trusted with handling what God has given you, then who will trust you with the things of God? At the end of the passage Jesus says this:

Luke 16:13:

"No one can serve two masters. Either you will hate the one and love the other, or you will be devoted to the one and despise the other. You cannot serve both God and money."

After Jesus said this, the Pharisees, who loved money, sneered at Him. They knew He was talking to them. He had hit the nail on the head.

Gem: We need to be wise with our money, our friendships and with the things of God. He trusts us to do the right thing and for us to build the kingdom of God with what we have.

What does it mean to "heap burning coals on their heads"?

> **Romans 12:20:**
>
> On the contrary: "If your enemy is hungry, feed him; if he is thirsty, give him something to drink. In doing this, you will heap burning coals on his head."

All of us want revenge! It makes us feel good when we think someone will get punished for doing us harm. But God says NO! What? We can't punish them? Our first thought is, that's not fair because we want them to suffer. But if we look at this passage we can see that God wants us to do the opposite.

Key: God's nature: He is love. Be kind to your enemy.

To understand this we have to think of the character of God. He is love and that means He wants the best for us; not just us but for everyone. He is also a just God and that means He is fair. We want to go out and hurt those who have hurt us and sometimes we feel that is justified and sometimes it isn't. But how do we know? When we are emotional and angry we may lash out at that person, maybe do even worse than they did, and that is sin. God's answer is to act in love.

1 Peter 3:9 says:

Do not repay evil with evil or insult with insult. On the contrary, repay evil with blessing, because to this you were called so that you may inherit a blessing.

It may seem strange but really God is looking out for us when He says this. He knows that if we lash out at our enemy we will sin. We could also confirm everything our enemy thought about us and it would not be a good witness to them. At every point of our lives we are to be a witness for Jesus, which means to show others that we are following Him and be a good example.

He wants us to be a blessing and if we are kind to these people they may be very puzzled! In fact, they may be blown away by it and want to hear what it is that makes us act that way. That helps us to talk to them about Jesus.

The Good News Bible translates it as "burn with shame" rather than coals, which could be a more accurate translation. They may be ashamed about what they have done and reconsider their actions. They may say sorry or think that mustn't happen again.

We must remember what it says in this verse:

Romans 12:19:

Do not take revenge, my dear friends, but leave room for God's wrath, for it is written: "It is mine to avenge; I will repay," says the Lord.

So whenever you are hurt by someone, take a deep breath and remember that God wants us to love our enemies, be kind to them, pray for them that they may find Him for themselves.

Gem: We mustn't act out of anger or revenge. We must be kind and caring, knowing that God will sort them out in His time.

Fascinating Fact:

Coal starts off as decayed plants in water. Over time it becomes buried by sediments and changes into coal. It is mainly carbon but has other elements in it too. Coal can be burned for heat or to make electricity, and has many by-products including soap, medicine, dyes, plastics and fibres.

Can everyone who works for Jesus go to heaven?

Matthew 7:21–23:

"Not everyone who says to me, 'Lord, Lord,' will enter the kingdom of heaven, but only the one who does the will of my Father who is in heaven. Many will say to me on that day, 'Lord, Lord, did we not prophesy in your name and in your name drive out demons and in your name perform many miracles?' Then I will tell them plainly, 'I never knew you. Away from me, you evildoers!'"

This has to be high up there on the list of the Bible's most puzzling passages. This is Jesus talking, and He's telling His disciples that not everyone who does things for Him will enter into heaven. Now you would think that anyone who performed miracles and had other special gifts would have to have the Holy Spirit. And if people said things in the name of Jesus that would be all they need, as it's not us, but Jesus, who has the powerful name.

Key: Looking at the paragraph before and after shows the theme of what Jesus was talking about. When they say that they had prophesied in His name, He said they were evil.

Looking at the paragraph before, it speaks about false prophets and that you would know them by their fruit, whether it is good or bad. The "fruit" is their actions. So people may appear to be doing things for God but, in reality, they are not. They are deceiving people.

The paragraph afterwards speaks about the builders building their houses on the sand and the rock. The one who builds on the rock – which is Jesus's words – will have a solid Christian life. The one who builds on the sand will listen but not do what Jesus says and will fall away from the Christian way when tough times come.

So from these two paragraphs we can see that Jesus is telling us that genuine people, who believe in Him, will live for Him and have good hearts and good motives. But there will be people who pretend to be believers but, in actual fact, their motives are far from pure and they can actually mislead people. They may be able to do all the miracles and cast out demons but they will never get into heaven because they are not following God.

> **Fascinating Fact:**
> The disciple Peter did many miracles including:
> - Healing a crippled man who got up and walked.
> - People were healed when his shadow fell on them.
> - A man who had been bedridden for eight years, got up, picked up his mat and walked.
> - He prayed for Dorcas, who had died, and she came back to life.

We see a good example of this in **Acts 8**. A man called Simon, who was a sorcerer (someone who practised magic), boasted about how great he was! Some people even believed he was from God. Now Philip, the disciple, came and told people the good news about Jesus and they believed and were baptised, including Simon. After this, Peter and John came down to the place where they were, Samaria, from Jerusalem, and prayed for people to receive the Holy Spirit by laying their hands on them. Look what happened next...

Acts 8:18–24:

When Simon saw that the Spirit was given at the laying on of the apostles' hands, he offered them money and said, "Give me also this ability so that everyone on whom I lay my hands may receive the Holy Spirit."

Peter answered: "May your money perish with you, because you thought you could buy the gift of God with money! You have no part or share in this ministry, because your heart is not right before God. Repent of this wickedness and pray to the Lord in the hope that he may forgive you for having such a thought in your heart. For I see that you are full of bitterness and captive to sin."

Then Simon answered, "Pray to the Lord for me so that nothing you have said may happen to me."

Peter and John were also called "apostles" and when they laid their hands on top of people's heads, the Holy Spirit came onto the people. Something spectacular must have happened as Simon offered money to be able to do it. Peter rightly told him that he couldn't buy the gift of God with money. We can see that Simon's heart was not right before God, but he had accepted Jesus and been baptised, so from the outside he looked like a Christian.

We don't know what happened to Simon, and hopefully he did repent and went on to live a Christian life, but it is a good example of how important it is to have our hearts right before God. So we can see that it is not our actions that get us into heaven but our relationship with Him. We can do wonderful things but if we don't know Jesus then it is all for nothing.

Gem: Getting to know God and Jesus is more important than doing amazing things to show off to others.

Is there such a thing as an "unforgivable sin"?

> **Mark 3:28–29:**
>
> "Truly I tell you, people can be forgiven all their sins and every slander they utter, but whoever blasphemes against the Holy Spirit will never be forgiven; they are guilty of an eternal sin."

It wasn't long after I became a Christian that I came across this verse. Oh no, I thought, what if I've done it already? What if I can't go to heaven because I have committed the unforgivable sin? I got really upset. The very sound of the word "unforgivable" puts fear into us! It sounds so final; no coming back from it.

Key: Reading the passage above tells us that it is those people who blaspheme against the Holy Spirit. To understand the word "blaspheme" and how it affects our relationship with the Holy Spirit.

People imagine all sorts of sin (that's doing wrong things) that can't be forgiven by God: murder, stealing, lying, even pulling out your sister's hair! Yes, these are all sins but, believe it or not, they can all be forgiven. In the Old Testament there was a man called Abraham who told lies about his wife, saying she was his sister. Not once but twice! Moses, also in the Old Testament, murdered someone, and yet they are both in God's Hall of Faith. (We can read this in Hebrews 11 in the New Testament.) They both became great men of God. So what is the sin that can't be forgiven? Puzzling, eh?!

In this particular verse Jesus was talking to the Pharisees, holy men who were righteous (doing the right thing) in their own eyes but not in God's eyes. It looked like they had it all together but Jesus said no, you look good on the outside but inside, in your heart, you don't love God, just yourself. They had seen Jesus do a miracle but they said He did it, not with the Holy Spirit, but in league with the devil. You can see how that offends

God! Sadly, they were rejecting God's free gift of salvation in Jesus. The word "blaspheme" means to disrespect God and not give Him the honour He is due, which is what the Pharisees did.

So if you love God and have given your life to Jesus, there is no way you have committed the unforgivable sin because when we invite God into our lives we are not rejecting Him but accepting Him. Great news! In fact they say if you are worried you've committed the unforgivable sin then you haven't, because you're concerned that you've offended God. The Bible tells us that we aren't going to be told off by God and that we aren't guilty once we believe in Jesus.

Romans 8:1:

Therefore, there is now no condemnation for those who are in Christ Jesus.

The people who commit the sin won't care because they've gone so far away from God that they won't worry about it. They have hardened their heart by becoming stubborn and not caring about God. They can have pride, arrogance and selfishness in their hearts instead of love, faith and kindness.

> **Fascinating Fact:**
> In the Old Testament there are 613 laws for people to keep in the Torah (the books of Moses); 365 of them say "do not" – one for each day of the year!

Gem: As long as we don't harden our heart towards Jesus we can't commit the unforgivable sin.

Be your own Bible Detective!

Now that you have seen how we unpicked our puzzling passages, you can do your own. In this book I have only just touched the surface; there are so many more to solve. Do you know you live in the best generation for information – ever! There are so many online resources open to you, including:

- Bible commentaries
- Bible concordances
- Websites
- YouTube

This is amazing, but nothing can beat having your own personal teacher – the Holy Spirit. He knows more than people can ever know.

How do you get started?

First, decide on a passage. As there are so many, that's not as easy as it sounds! You may already have one in mind but, if not, you could choose a topic such as love, hope or faith. Put it into your search engine and see what comes up. Or you can read some Bible stories and see if any of them are puzzling to you. Or you can put "puzzling Bible verses" into search and that will give you quite a few!

Secondly, we need to ask the Holy Spirit to help us. God wrote the Bible, through men, and so He is the best person to give us wisdom about our passage.

You can pray a prayer similar to this one:

Dear Holy Spirit,

Please help me to understand this passage. Guide me as I read and study, and show me what You want me to learn from it.

In Jesus' name, Amen.

What's next?

Then read and reread the passage several times. Write down anything that stands out to you that the Holy Spirit is showing you. Keep looking for that all important key. What is it that helps you unlock the passage? It might be a key word, or you may have to read the Bible verses before or after it. We call this "context", which is very important. If we take things out of context then we can get a meaning that is totally wrong. For example, in Romans Paul writes:

Romans 7:19:

For I do not do the good I want to do, but the evil I do not want to do – this I keep on doing.

Now this sounds like an excuse for keeping on doing bad things! But if we look further on in the passage we can see that Paul is saying that he realises that even though he *wants* to do good things, he keeps doing bad things. So can we do bad stuff too? Further investigation into **Romans 7** makes it clear that no, we can't, but we have a battle that rages in us and we have to keep being aware of it. Paul had to resist and live the life that Jesus wanted him to live. A different thing entirely!

When this is done, you can begin your research. Online Bibles often have study tools to help you. You can pop the verse into the search bar and see what comes up. Obviously, you have to be careful about what you read on the internet, and if you're not sure ask an adult. You can also read Bibles that you may find in the library, which have study notes and concordances. You can also get commentaries online from other people who have studied the passage before you.

As you continue to research and make notes, don't forget to pray every so often. Even though you prayed at the beginning, it's good to pray at intervals, and afterwards listen quietly to see if God is speaking to you. Sometimes you can leave it for a few days and come back to it and things may pop out at you that you haven't seen before.

When I was young I remember that I was so puzzled about the plank and the speck. It just didn't make sense. I didn't pray or research it at the time but when I was older, and I had become a Christian, I prayed and the Holy Spirit helped me to understand it. So obvious once you know!

Reading the Bible will help you grow as a Christian and enable you to live the life that Jesus wants you to live. Once you start to read and find out more from the Bible then it's important to apply it to your life. We hear from James:

James 1:22–25:

Do not merely listen to the word, and so deceive yourselves. Do what it says. Anyone who listens to the word but does not do what it says is like someone who looks at his face in a mirror and, after looking at himself, goes away and immediately forgets what he looks like. But whoever looks intently into the perfect law that gives freedom and continues in it – not forgetting what they have heard but doing it – they will be blessed in what they do.

In other words, we need to put what we read into practice and then we can live God's way and be blessed and be a blessing to others.

In **Acts 17:11** we read:

Now the Berean Jews were of more noble character than those in Thessalonica, for they received the message with great eagerness and examined the Scriptures every day to see if what Paul said was true.

We can learn a lot from the Berean Jews…
Firstly, they were excited about God's Word.
Secondly, they worked together as a group.
Thirdly, they made sure that everything Paul said was true, and that he wasn't "making it up".

It's good to be excited about God's Word! It is the blueprint for our lives, a map that can guide us to be the very best that we can be. It's also good to study with others, as well as doing it on our own. Most churches have groups where you can learn together, and there are youth groups too.

The third point is very important. I can't finish this book without giving you a warning about false teachers. This happened to me and it wasn't an easy thing to go through, and I don't want it to happen to you.

Warning

Please, please be careful. I can't emphasise enough that there are people who are not true Christians but will tell you that they are. The Bible tells us "many will come in my name", which means there will be a lot of people who will claim to be Jesus but they aren't. Believe me, when Jesus comes back, as He says He will, then we will know about it! He will come back in glory. Sadly, there are groups who will claim to be the only ones who can get you to heaven, and these are called "cults".

How do I know if it's a cult?

They will not have the true gospel. They will alter what God says in His Word, the Bible, and say that some things aren't right that normal

Christians believe in. They will try and separate you from family and friends, so that you have to rely on them. Some cults have books that they add to the Bible to explain their version of what it means. Also, any type of control is wrong. If people are trying to force you to believe what they think, or offer lots of empty promises, then they could well be a cult. God never forces us, He always lets us make our own decisions.

So like the Bereans, test everything that you are told by God's Word. It's like checking the answers when you've done maths, so you know they are right. If someone tells you something about God, then check in the Bible to see if it's right.

I hope that you will enjoy studying what God has to say to us and that you will find lots of answers to those puzzling passages of Scripture. One day you may even write a book of your own.

Can you find some of the characters from the book in the picture below?

Happy detecting!

Glossary

Altar: The word altar means "place of sacrifice" and was often made of stones or wood and sometimes covered in brass or gold. People would kill an animal on it and offer it to God.

Amorites: These were a group of people who were fierce warriors who lived in Canaan, the land God wanted for the Israelites. They were a wicked people who did very bad things and worshipped false gods.

Angel of the Lord: In the Old Testament the Angel of the Lord is mentioned many times, and he would speak to humans on God's behalf. It is believed he could be Jesus, even though Jesus wasn't born yet and it sounds impossible, because He was with God from the beginning.

Angels: Angels are messengers sent from God to help people and to give messages. They can appear on their own or with others. The Bible tells us that there are good angels who love God and fallen ones who work alongside Satan.

Baal: Baal was a false god who was worshipped by the Canaanites and was the god of the sun, rain, fertility and agriculture.

Baptise: In Acts 2:38, Peter says, "Repent and be baptised, every one of you, in the name of Jesus Christ for the forgiveness of your sins." When someone is baptised they are immersed in water and their sins are symbolically washed away. Just like Jesus we are dying to our old selves and being resurrected into a new life.

Bible: This is God's Word. He inspired over 40 writers to write 66 books which were put into one big book. It is divided into the Old and New Testaments. The Old has 39 books and the New 27 books. It tells how God made the world and how He rescued people from their sins by sending Jesus.

Canaan: This was the land that God gave to Abraham to be the home of the Israelites, His chosen people. God asked them to cleanse the land by getting rid of all the people who lived there, because they were doing wicked things.

Commandments: God gave the Israelites ten commandments when they left Egypt. These were rules for them to help them to live peacefully with each other. They were to love God and each other and not to do bad things like kill and steal.

Commentaries: These are comments from people who have studied the Bible and they give you information on the meaning of the passage or some background to it.

Concordance: This can help you to find a passage in the Bible, even if you can only remember one word. It can also help you find where else in the Bible that word occurs and even what it means from the Hebrew and Greek. Some Bibles have them at the back or you can find them online or in book shops.

Conundrum: A conundrum is a difficult problem to solve, a riddle or a puzzle.

Covenant: A covenant is an agreement or a promise between God and His people. In the New Testament the covenant is that God will forgive sins when people put their faith in Jesus, God's Son. Jesus died for our sins.

Crucified: This was a cruel way the Romans used to kill people who were criminals. Firstly the person was beaten, then they carried their cross to the place of execution, and finally they were nailed to the cross and died a very slow death, sometimes taking several days.

Curse: A curse is made by a person who wants bad things to happen to someone else saying they wish they were hurt in some way. A curse is the opposite to a blessing.

Devil and demons: God is the creator of everything, including the devil. God is love and He is good whereas the devil is bad and full of pride and hate. The devil and his demons, fallen angels, try to get people to sin and stop them from having a relationship with God.

Enemy, the: Our enemy, as Christians, is the devil. He will do anything to stop you making a commitment to Jesus, and if you do, he will do everything he can to make you turn away from Him. But the good news is, God is more powerful than the devil and has defeated him.

Eternity, heaven and hell: Heaven and hell are real places. Heaven is full of love and praise to God and God has His throne there. Hell is described in the Bible as dark, a gnashing of teeth and fire; a place where you are separated from God for all eternity. Eternity means it goes on forever and ever without end.

Faith: Faith is believing in something that you cannot see but know to be true. We need to have faith to believe in God and the Bible and to put our trust in Jesus.

False gods: These are also called idols and are objects, often made of stone, metal or wood, that are worshipped and, in the Old Testament, sacrifices were made to them. Often people believed that making these gods happy would bring them luck, good crops and lots of children. When the Israelites turned away from God to worship these gods, it made God very jealous and angry.

Forgiveness: This is what we have to do when other people hurt us. It is an act of will, not of emotions, and we have to ask God to help us forgive others and let them off the hook, even if they are not sorry.

Fruit of the Spirit: This refers to the Holy Spirit and what comes from Him when we let Him into our lives. The fruit are things we need to walk the Christian way and they are: love, joy, peace, patience, kindness, goodness, faithfulness, gentleness and self-control.

God's Kingdom: A kingdom is where the king is in charge. So in God's Kingdom, He is in charge and rules over it. Jesus told lots of parables about the Kingdom, and how wonderful and precious it was. He also said that when we believed in Him, the Kingdom was in us too.

Grace: Grace is having something wonderful given to us that we don't deserve to have. God has saved us from our sins, even though we haven't done anything to earn it.

Healing: When Jesus died on the cross, He died for our sins and the Bible tells us that He also died to make us well. So Jesus can heal us from illness, both physical and emotional. When He was on earth He went around healing people, so the blind could see and the deaf could hear.

Holy Spirit: The Holy Spirit is part of the Trinity – God the Father, God the Son, and God the Holy Spirit. When Jesus left this earth He told us He would send the Holy Spirit, who is our comforter and the Spirit of truth. He is a person and can bring us into a full relationship with God.

Idiom: This is a sentence that means something different to what we say, such as "Hold your horses"'. We're not saying hold onto some horses, we mean "Stop, don't rush into it".

Jews: When Abraham became a nation, they were called Israelites after his son, Israel. Hundreds of years later the nation divided into two: Judah and Israel. After some time Israel was scattered and Judah remained, and the Jews are called after Judah.

Mercy: When God shows us mercy, He is showing us compassion and love, even though we have done wrong things. He wants us to show mercy to others too, not just those we love but also our enemies.

New Testament: Testament means an agreement between God and man. The Bible is divided into two: Old and New. In the New we learn about Jesus and how He can save us from our sins.

Old Testament: The first part of the Bible is the Old Testament and this tells us how God made the world, how the nation of Israel came into being and what He did to try and show people how to love and follow Him.

Pagans: A pagan is someone who doesn't worship God but other gods or nature. In the Bible non-Jews or Gentiles were people who weren't born a Jew and could be thought of as a pagan.

Parable: These are short stories that help you to understand a religious or moral truth. Jesus told a lot of parables and linked them with everyday things, which would help people to understand them. An example is the Lost Sheep, as people knew a lot about shepherds and their sheep, and the truth of the parable is that God loves everyone, and He looks for them when they go astray.

Persecute: When people are persecuted they are punished by others because of what they believe in.

Pharisees: These were Jewish people who believed in God and told others what to do but often didn't do these things themselves. Jesus called them blind guides. He said that on the outside they looked good, but inside they were far from God and only wanted to please themselves. Not all Pharisees, however, were bad. Some, like Nicodemus, believed Jesus was sent from God.

Prophet: This was someone sent by God to tell the people His messages. Prophets were often treated badly by the Israelites, even killed. There were good prophets but there were also bad prophets, often called false prophets, because they told people what they wanted to hear rather than the truth.

Repent: This is what people do when they are truly sorry for their sins, and want to turn away from the wrong things they have done. They come before God and say sorry for what they have done and they won't do it again. It wouldn't be repentance if you said sorry for stealing, and then went back and stole again the next day. You have to say it, and mean it.

Sacrifice: This is when something, usually an animal, is killed as an offering to God or a god, to bring about a good event such as a harvest. In the Old Testament it was instead of people being punished for their sins. It can also mean giving up something that you really love for a better cause. Jesus was the ultimate sacrifice when He died on the cross for our sins, so that we can have a relationship with God.

Salvation: Salvation means getting right with God. Our sins get in the way of us having a relationship with God because God is holy and can't accept sin. The punishment for sin is death! God in His mercy allowed Jesus, instead of us, to be killed, meaning we could be rescued from our sin. We can be saved if we believe in Jesus with our whole heart.

Scribes: These were men who wrote out the Bible and other documents and had a good knowledge of the law.

Self-righteous: These are people who think they are better than everyone else and can do no wrong, often judging others. Jesus called the Pharisees self-righteous.

Sin: Sin is doing the opposite of what God wants, disobeying Him and doing things our own way. This causes a barrier between us and God. When Adam ate the fruit of the tree of the knowledge of good and evil, he disobeyed God; sin entered the world as a result.

Spirit, the: This is the Holy Spirit, God's Spirit that also lives in us once we have accepted Jesus as our saviour. We are made up of body, soul and spirit and we connect with God through our spirit.

Spiritual battle: When we become Christians we enter into a battle with the devil and he will always try and get us to disobey God. We have lots of tools to help us in our fight: prayer, God's Word, armour and fellow Christians.

Trinity: The Trinity is made up of three persons in one God. God the Father, God the Son and God the Holy Spirit. This is a difficult concept to understand. The way I describe it is an egg has a shell, a white and a yolk, yet it is one egg. God the Father, Son and Holy Spirit are separate but there is only one God.

Witness: When we witness to others we are telling them about Jesus and what He has done for us. We are also a witness by the lives we live. If we did things that were upsetting to God, like swearing, then that would be a bad witness. If we did things that were pleasing to God, that would be a good witness to others.

Word, the: This is God's Word and can mean the Bible but also Jesus was described as the Word in John 1:1: "In the beginning was the Word, and the Word was with God and the Word was God."

Worship: This is an act of praise that we give to God because He is holy and has given us everything, including His own Son. We can worship in many different ways: singing, praying, reading the Bible, serving others and going to church are some of the things we can do.

Helpful resources

I wouldn't have been able to explain the puzzling passages in this book without the help of the Holy Spirit and a lot of research. Some of the websites that I found particularly helpful were:

Gotquestions.org – this has just about every Bible topic under the sun and includes some videos too. Their kids' version is gqkidz.org – you can ask them any question you want and they will answer it.

Christianity.com – this includes fun Bible games.

Answersingenesis.org/kids – this has activities and videos plus lots about creation.

Dltk-kids.com – tells Bible stories and gives you lots of crafts to make too.

Crossroadskidsclub.net – gives you God's story. Crossroads Kids' Club is also on YouTube. The videos are such fun, and have a quick version at the end – just in case you missed it!

Superbook.cbn.com – this has lots of videos of Bible stories and fun games, all introduced by Gizmo the robot.

There are many online Bibles, concordances and commentaries that are free to use including:

Biblehub.com/childrens – choose lots of Bible stories from the list.

Biblegateway.com

Biblestudytools.com

Acknowledgements

After writing my first book, *Gospel in a Nutshell*, I didn't think the second book would be as exciting – but I was wrong! It's been a real joy to bring this book, *Puzzling Passages*, to life and I've enjoyed working out the answers to some of the Bible's most confusing verses.

As always, this book would not have been at its best without the help and support of so many people. My thanks and gratitude go to the following people who have helped me and *Puzzling Passages* on its journey:

Once again, I've teamed up with the delightful Kate Hobbs and she has illustrated it with her amazing and colourful art work. At the age of only eighteen you'll agree that she's done a brilliant job.

Rachael, for putting in all the hard work of fitting the book together, along with Karen and all at Verité CM publishing. Thank you for being so patient with me!

Thanks to Louise for her editing and making this a manuscript that is polished and professional.

Thanks to Martin, Vicky, Paul, Sophie and Matt. Their input has been so valuable, helping me to question my work and make sure I don't make any mistakes.

Thank you to my dear family and friends who gave me support and encouragement along the way. It means so much.

And to you my readers, thank you for reading this book. There is no point producing a book unless it is going to be read! My heartfelt prayer is that you will not only read it but take it and build upon it and live fruitful lives for Him.

Endorsements

*"I really liked Trisha's first book **Gospel in a Nutshell**. It was great. I had fun looking for the hidden snails and the stories were easy to understand and read. If you haven't already read it I would recommend that you do."*

Daniel, aged 9

Tricia's first book was absolutely amazing. It talks about God and Jesus. My favourite part of the story is when Jesus was against a lot of people who were protesting against Him. This book has lots of interesting facts of God which I'd like to tell my friends and family. I learnt from the drawings about Jesus and how He was born, died on the cross and even made people get healed. May the Lord bless you.

Munesu, aged 8

---

*I have found **Gospel in a Nutshell** to be clear and simple to follow and understand as I had never really delved deeply into Christianity. Anyone new to the subject, young or old, would find this an exciting start to want to explore and discover the Bible stories in more depth. I found it difficult to read the Bible as it was in old-style language. Trisha's book is a breath of fresh air.*

Shirley

About the Author

Trisha enjoys writing and has published many articles in magazines. It was a dream come true to publish her first book, *Gospel in a Nutshell*, which inspired her to write *Puzzling Passages*. She has worked with children and young people for over 30 years, as well as having a family of her own. As an author she loves that she can combine her faith, her writing and her love for young people and produce something of eternal value.

About the Illustrator

Puzzling Passages is Kate's second book following on from *Gospel in a Nutshell*. She enjoys bringing Bible stories to life in a bright and colourful way. Her favourite chapter to illustrate in *Puzzling Passages* was "What does the number 666 stand for?". She is an inspiration to other young would-be illustrators.

Now eighteen, Kate plans to study Classics and a bit of French at the University of Kent while still hoping to continue her illustrating.

Also by Trisha Foote

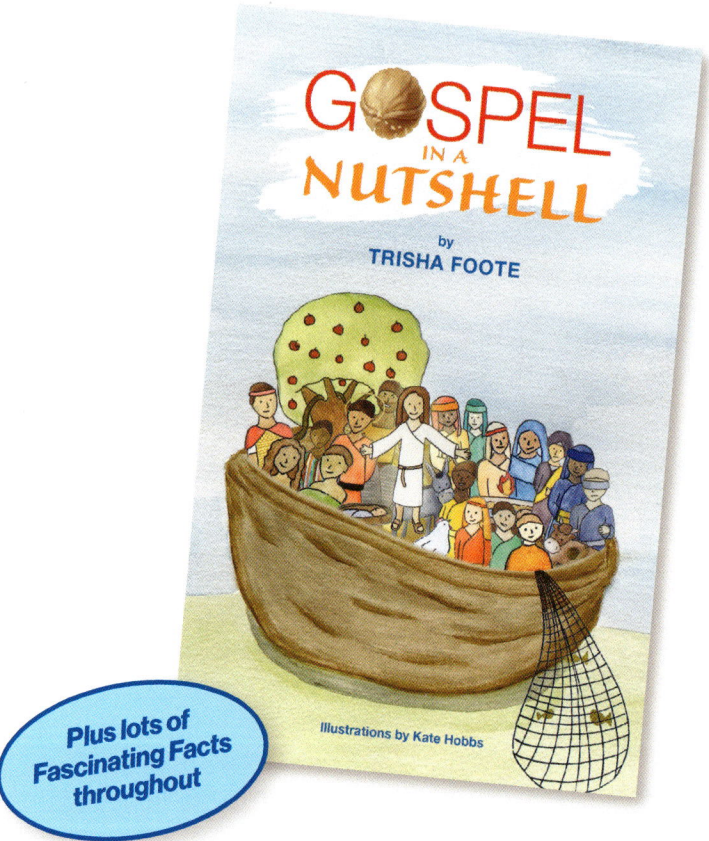

**Is the Bible just a lot of stories put together?
Or is there something more?
Does it answer life's big questions?**
"What is the point of life?"
"Can I live my best life possible?"
"Is God real?"
"Can it tell us how life began and what will happen
at the end of time?"
Curious? Well, take a look inside 'Gospel in a Nutshell' and see…
Come on an amazing journey with me!